THE PERFECT
EGG COOKBOOK

THE PERFECT EGG COOKBOOK

OVER 90 RECIPES FOR OMELETTES, PANCAKES, SOUFFLÉS, CUSTARDS, MERINGUES, CAKES, SOUPS AND MORE, WITH OVER 350 STEP-BY-STEP PHOTOGRAPHS

ALEX BARKER

HERMES
HOUSE

This edition is published by Hermes House, an imprint of Anness Publishing Ltd, Hermes House,
88–89 Blackfriars Road, London SE1 8HA; tel. 020 7401 2077; fax 020 7633 9499

www.hermeshouse.com; www.annesspublishing.com

If you like the images in this book and would like to investigate using them for publishing, promotions or advertising,
please visit our website www.practicalpictures.com for more information.

Publisher: Joanna Lorenz
Managing Editor: Linda Fraser
Editor: Susannah Blake
Editorial Reader: Jonathan Marshall
Designer: Nigel Partridge
Photography: Amanda Heywood (recipes) and Steve Moss (reference)
Food for Photography: Joy Skipper (recipes) and Alex Barker and Stephanie England (reference)

ETHICAL TRADING POLICY

At Anness Publishing we believe that business should be conducted in an ethical and ecologically sustainable way, with respect for the
environment and a proper regard to the replacement of the natural resources we employ.
As a publisher, we use a lot of wood pulp in high-quality paper for printing, and that wood commonly comes from spruce trees. We are
therefore currently growing more than 750,000 trees in three Scottish forest plantations: Berrymoss (130 hectares/320 acres),
West Touxhill (125 hectares/305 acres) and Deveron Forest (75 hectares/185 acres). The forests we manage contain more than
3.5 times the number of trees employed each year in making paper for the books we manufacture.
Because of this ongoing ecological investment programme, you, as our customer, can have the pleasure and reassurance of knowing that
a tree is being cultivated on your behalf to naturally replace the materials used to make the book you are holding.
For further information about this scheme, go to www.annesspublishing.com/trees

PUBLISHER'S NOTE

Although the advice and information in this book are believed to be accurate and true at the time of going to press, neither the authors
nor the publisher can accept any legal responsibility or liability for any errors or omissions that may have been made nor for any
inaccuracies nor for any loss, harm or injury that comes about from following instructions or advice in this book.
The very young, the elderly, pregnant women and those in ill-health or with a compromised immune system are advised against
consuming raw eggs or dishes and drinks containing raw eggs.

NOTES

Bracketed terms are intended for American readers.
For all recipes, quantities are given in both metric and imperial measures and, where appropriate, in standard cups and spoons.
Follow one set of measures, but not a mixture, because they are not interchangeable.
Standard spoon and cup measures are level. 1 tsp = 5ml, 1 tbsp = 15ml, 1 cup = 250ml/8fl oz.
Australian standard tablespoons are 20ml. Australian readers should use 3 tsp in place of 1 tbsp for measuring small quantities.
American pints are 16fl oz/2 cups. American readers should use 20fl oz/2.5 cups in place of 1 pint when measuring liquids.
Electric oven temperatures in this book are for conventional ovens. When using a fan oven, the temperature will probably need to be
reduced by about 10–20°C/20–40°F. Since ovens vary, you should check with your manufacturer's instruction book for guidance.
Medium (US large) eggs are used unless otherwise stated.

Main front cover image shows Cheese and Onion Flan – for recipe, see page 50.

Previously published as *Take One Egg...*

CONTENTS

EGG BASICS

Eggs are one of nature's convenience foods: neatly "packaged" in single portions, readily available, inexpensive and easily digested. They are packed with protein and contain vitamins A, B and D and important minerals such as iron and calcium. They are wonderfully versatile, form the basis of a vast range of savoury and sweet dishes, and make a quick and tasty meal if served on their own or with a simple vegetable accompaniment. Eggs are used in cuisines throughout the world and are popular with both children and adults. Ideal for vegetarians and meat-eaters alike, the egg is every cook's stand-by.

GRADING

Eggs are graded and checked at the packing station. A light is shone through them so the contents can be checked without cracking the shell. Any eggs that have imperfections are removed.

Only grade A (EU) or grade A and AA (US) eggs reach the stores. In the US,

eggs are washed and, as this removes their protective bloom, a light mineral oil is usually applied before packing. This is not permitted in the EU.

SIZING

Eggs are sized according to weight. Size does not make any difference when you are cooking eggs individually, for example when frying, poaching or boiling them. However, in baking, the size of egg can be important because the success of many recipes depends on accurate proportions of ingredients.

DATE MARKING

Producers outside EU or US inspection areas are governed by laws in their own country or state. In the EU and US, all boxes of eggs are date marked. The date of packing is used in the US. Each day of the year has a number: 1 refers to eggs packed on 1 January and 365 refers to those packed on 31 December. Boxes may also carry an expiry date

Above: Eggs should be stored unwashed and with the pointed end down to reduce evaporation.

after which the eggs cannot be sold. This "best before" date allows for seven days after purchase when the eggs are safe to eat. The laying date and "sell by" or packing date can be stamped on the shells in the EU and US.

CHOOSING AND STORING EGGS

With the existing quality controls, there is little need for thorough checking, but it is worth making sure that the eggs are intact and not cracked. Also check the date stamped on the box or eggs. Try to buy from a store with a fast turnover so that the eggs are fresh. Avoid buying eggs that are already two weeks old.

Egg shells are porous, so eggs are vulnerable to bacteria and can absorb odours, which may affect their flavour. Always store in an egg compartment in the refrigerator at or below 4°C/40°F, where fresh eggs can be kept safely for 3–4 weeks.

Remove eggs from the refrigerator a short while before using them for cooking, especially when making meringues or other whisked dishes, as a better result is often achieved if the eggs are at room temperature.

Left: Although there are a large number of edible bird's eggs, the majority of eggs used in the kitchen are hen's eggs.

SIMPLE COOKING TECHNIQUES

Eggs are delicious when combined with other ingredients, but they are also very good cooked on their own. The basic techniques of egg cooking are easy to master and will help you with more complex methods and mixtures.

SEPARATING EGGS

Many egg dishes, such as soufflés and meringues, require the yolk and white to be separated.

1 To crack the egg, using a single, sharp movement, tap the egg firmly on the side of the bowl as near to the middle of the shell as possible. Alternatively, make an indent in the shell by tapping the egg with the blade of a knife.

2 Use your thumbs to prise the shell halves apart gently, trying to break the shell as little as you possibly can. Turn the shell half containing the yolk upright and let the white from both halves drop into the bowl below.

3 Tilt the shell halves to slip the yolk from one to the other, being careful not to break it. Let the excess white fall into the bowl. Repeat until most of the white has been transferred to the bowl. Slip the yolk into a second bowl and check that there is no white left in the shell.

BOILING EGGS

Eggs are delicious soft-boiled (soft-cooked) and eaten on their own for breakfast or hard-boiled and in used in salads and as a sandwich filling.

1 When cooking chilled eggs, it is best to put them into a pan of cold water.

2 Alternatively, lower the eggs on a spoon into simmering water, taking care not to let them drop on to the base of the pan or they will crack.

3 Heat the water until bubbling gently, then begin timing the cooking, using the table below.

Cooking times
This is a guide to cooking eggs added to hot water. Start timing when the water boils gently. Reduce the time for eggs added to cold water by about 30 seconds.

Cooking time in minutes

	*Small	Medium	Large
Soft	3	4	4½–5
Semi-firm	4	5–6	6–7
(yolks still soft)			
Hard	7	8–10	10–12

*(US medium, large and extra large)

POACHING EGGS

This simple cooking method produces a delicious egg with a wonderful, soft texture. Poached eggs can be enjoyed on their own, in salads or as part of a dish, such as eggs Florentine.

1 Pour about 2.5–4cm/1–1½in water into a frying pan. Add 15ml/1 tbsp vinegar and bring to the boil. Reduce the heat to a gentle simmer. Crack the egg into a cup or small dish so that you can control its position easily when adding it to the pan, then gently tip it into the bubbling water.

2 Cook the egg very gently for 1 minute undisturbed, then gently spoon a little water over the centre to cook the yolk.

3 Use a skimmer, slotted spoon or fish slice (spatula) to lift out the egg.

CODDLING EGGS

This gentle cooking method cooks gives delicate results and cooks eggs evenly. To coddle in the shell, add eggs to the pan as for boiling and bring the water to a gentle boil, then cover and remove the pan from the heat. Leave the eggs to stand for about 5 minutes for a soft egg or 7 minutes for a firmer set.

Using an Egg Coddler

Butter the dish and crack an egg into it. Season, replace the lid and put in a pan of simmering water for 6–10 minutes, depending on the size of the egg. For a very soft egg, turn off the heat and leave to stand for 6–10 minutes.

BAKING EGGS

Delicate, oven-baked eggs are quick and easy to prepare and can be flavoured with a variety of ingredients. Cover the eggs with foil to prevent the yolks from overcooking.

1 Preheat the oven to 180°C/350°F/ Gas 4. Lightly butter some ramekins and crack an egg into each. Top with a knob (pat) of butter and season.

2 Stand the ramekins in a roasting pan, half filled with hot water. Bake for about 15 minutes, or until the whites are set.

FRYING EGGS

Eggs can be shallow fried or deep-fried. Shallow frying with little or no oil is the healthier method, but when deep-fried briefly and well drained, eggs are wonderfully crisp. The fat must be hot enough for the eggs to bubble and cook as soon as they are added to the pan, but not so hot that they break up.

Shallow Frying Eggs

1 Heat 30–45ml/2–3 tbsp oil in a heavy frying pan over a medium heat. Crack the egg into the pan and allow it to settle and start bubbling gently around the edges before basting with hot oil or adding another egg.

2 After 1 minute, spoon a little hot oil over the yolk to cook the egg evenly.

3 Cook for a further 1 minute, until the white has become totally opaque and the edges are just turning brown. For a firmer yolk, cook the egg for a further minute. Lift the egg out of the pan, with a fish slice (spatula), carefully draining off the oil.

4 Alternatively, if you would prefer a firmer, crisper egg still, gently flip the egg over, using a fish slice, and cook for a further minute on the other side.

Deep-frying Eggs

1 Crack the egg into a cup or small bowl so that you can slip it quickly and easily into the pan without splashing yourself with hot oil or breaking up the egg yolk.

2 Heat about 2.5cm/1in vegetable or sunflower oil in a deep frying pan to 180°C/350°F, or until it is hot enough to turn a cube of day-old bread brown in about 45 seconds. Gently tip the egg into the hot oil.

3 Cook the egg for 30 seconds, then use a slotted spoon to turn or fold it over carefully.

4 Cook for a further 30 seconds, or until the egg white is crisp and golden on both sides. Remove with a slotted spoon and drain on kitchen paper.

SCRAMBLING EGGS

Lightly beaten eggs are gently stirred in hot butter until they set. They can be soft and creamy or cooked until firm and dry. Milk or water may be added.

Making Scrambled Eggs

1 Lightly beat 3 eggs per serving and season to taste. Heat 15g/½oz/1 tbsp butter in a small non-stick pan until sizzling. Pour in the eggs and stir.

2 Stir frequently over a medium heat for 1–2 minutes until the eggs are lightly set but still very moist and creamy.

3 For more firmly set scrambled egg, stir less frequently for about 4 minutes.

4 For a chunkier texture, stir the eggs occasionally with a flat-ended wooden spoon or spatula.

OMELETTES

Lightly beaten eggs, seasoned and fried to form a light omelette, provide a meal in about 3 minutes. Any number of seasonings, fillings or toppings can be added to make an omelette more substantial. Thick, set omelettes can be served cold, cut into small portions to make finger food. When the whites are whisked and folded into the yolks, a plain omelette is elevated to soufflé omelette status. With a rich fruit filling, soufflé omelettes make luxurious, yet light desserts.

Although special omelette pans are available, any heavy, medium-size, non-stick frying pan will do. Prepare the flavourings and fillings first. Have a warmed serving plate ready and do not cook the omelette until you are ready to eat it. Traditionally rolled or folded to enclose a filling, an omelette can also be served flat and topped with flavouring ingredients.

Making a Classic Omelette

1 Allow 3 eggs per omelette. In a bowl, lightly beat the eggs with seasonings.

2 Heat 15g/½ oz/1 tbsp butter in an omelette or frying pan until very hot and sizzling, but not smoking or browning. Pour in the eggs, tilting the pan slightly.

3 Cook the eggs for a few seconds until the base has set, then use a fork to push in the sides or stir gently. The idea is to ensure that the unset egg mixture runs on to the hot pan and starts cooking. Cook for about 1 minute, or until the egg is just beginning to set. For a firmer set, cook for a little longer.

4 Use a large flat spatula to fold over a third of the omelette.

5 Tilting the pan away from you, flip the omelette over again and immediately slide it out on to a warmed serving plate in a single smooth action.

COOK'S TIP

In a perfect omelette, the egg in the middle should still be slightly runny or creamy when served, but the omelette can be completely set if you like.

BREAKFASTS AND BRUNCHES

Eggs make a perfect start to the day, providing plenty of energy to keep you going. They first became important breakfast food in the Victorian era and have become a key ingredient, both for breakfasts and lazy weekend brunches, and are used to create enticing dishes that are a far cry from plain boiled eggs or poached eggs on toast. This chapter includes classic breakfast and brunch dishes, such as Poached Eggs Florentine, Chive Scrambled Eggs in Brioches, and Bacon, Egg and Chanterelle Baps, as well as contemporary recipes, such as Stuffed Thai Omelette, and Vegetable Pancakes with Tomato Salsa.

SAVOURY SCRAMBLED EGGS

ALSO KNOWN AS "SCOTCH WOODCOCK", THESE EGGS ARE FLAVOURED WITH A HINT OF ANCHOVY AND WERE POPULAR IN ENGLAND AT THE BEGINNING OF THE 20TH CENTURY. THEY WOULD HAVE BEEN SERVED AS A SAVOURY INSTEAD OF CHEESE AT THE END OF A MEAL, RATHER THAN FOR BREAKFAST.

SERVES TWO

INGREDIENTS

2 slices bread
40g/1½oz/3 tbsp butter, plus
  extra for spreading
anchovy paste, such as
  Gentleman's Relish, for spreading
2 eggs and 2 egg yolks, beaten
60–90ml/4–6 tbsp single (light)
  cream or milk
salt and ground black pepper
anchovy fillets, cut into strips,
  and paprika, to garnish

COOK'S TIP
These creamy scrambled eggs make a great brunch dish. Serve with a glass of crisp white wine and follow with a fresh fruit salad.

1 Toast the bread, spread with butter and anchovy paste, then remove the crusts and cut into triangles. Keep warm.

2 Melt the rest of the butter in a medium non-stick pan, then stir in the beaten eggs, cream or milk, and a little salt and pepper. Heat very gently, stirring constantly, until the mixture begins to thicken.

3 Remove the pan from the heat and continue to stir until the mixture becomes very creamy, but do not allow it to harden.

4 Divide the scrambled eggs among the triangles of toast and garnish each with strips of anchovy fillet and a generous sprinkling of paprika. Serve the eggs immediately, while still hot.

PIPÉRADE WITH CROSTINI

THIS MIXTURE OF SWEET PEPPERS, TOMATOES AND EGGS HAS ALL THE FLAVOURS OF THE MEDITERRANEAN. IT IS PERFECT FOR A LAZY WEEKEND BRUNCH OR A LIGHT LUNCHTIME SNACK.

SERVES SIX

INGREDIENTS
  60ml/4 tbsp bacon fat, duck fat
    or olive oil
  2 small onions, coarsely chopped
  4 red, orange or yellow (bell)
    peppers, seeded and chopped
  2 large garlic cloves, finely chopped
  pinch of chilli or hot cayenne pepper
  675g/1½lb ripe plum tomatoes,
    peeled, seeded and chopped
  15ml/1 tbsp chopped fresh oregano
    or 5ml/1 tsp dried
  1 long French stick
  60–90ml/4–6 tbsp olive oil
  25g/1oz/2 tbsp butter
  6 eggs, beaten
  salt and ground black pepper
  basil leaves, to serve

1 Heat the fat or oil in a large heavy frying pan. Add the onions and cook over a gentle heat, stirring occasionally, for about 5 minutes until softened but not coloured.

2 Add the peppers, garlic and chilli or cayenne. Cook for a further 5 minutes, stirring, then add the plum tomatoes, seasoning and oregano, and cook over a moderate heat for 15–20 minutes until the peppers are soft and most of the liquid has evaporated.

COOK'S TIP
To make a quick party version, cut the bread into thick slices and mix about 200ml/7fl oz/scant 1 cup ready-made sweet (bell) pepper and tomato pasta sauce into the eggs and continue as above.

3 Preheat the oven to 200°C/400°F/ Gas 6. Cut the bread in half lengthways, trim off the ends, then cut into six equal pieces and brush with olive oil. Place on baking sheets and bake for 8 minutes until crisp and just turning golden.

4 Heat the butter until it bubbles, add the eggs and stir until softly scrambled. Turn off the heat and stir in the pepper mixture. Divide evenly among the pieces of bread and sprinkle with the basil leaves. Serve hot or warm.

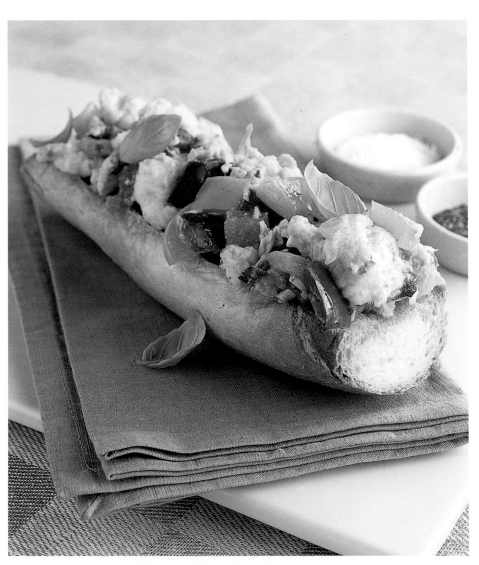

SWEET PERSIAN BREAKFAST OMELETTE

THIS VERSION OF A SIMPLE OMELETTE IS POPULAR THROUGHOUT THE MIDDLE EAST AND IS EXCELLENT EATEN WITH A FRUITY HOME-MADE JAM OR CONSERVE.

SERVES ONE

INGREDIENTS
   3 eggs
   10ml/2 tsp caster (superfine) sugar
   5ml/1 tsp plain (all-purpose) flour
   10g/¼oz/½ tbsp unsalted (sweet)
     butter
   bread and jam, to serve

COOK'S TIP
Continue the Middle Eastern theme when choosing a jam to serve with this omelette. Pick one made from fruits such as fig or apricot that are popular in the Middle East. Alternatively, you could use raspberry or strawberry jam.

1 Break the eggs into a large bowl, add the sugar and flour and beat until really frothy. Heat the butter in an omelette pan until it begins to bubble, then pour in the egg mixture and cook, without stirring, until it begins to set.

2 Run a wooden spatula around the edge of the omelette, then carefully turn it over and cook the second side for 1–2 minutes until golden. Serve hot or warm with thick slices of fresh bread and fruity jam.

CHIVE SCRAMBLED EGGS <u>IN</u> BRIOCHES

SCRAMBLED EGGS ARE DELICIOUS AT ANY TIME OF DAY BUT, WHEN SERVED WITH FRANCE'S FAVOURITE BREAKFAST BREAD, THEY BECOME THE ULTIMATE BREAKFAST OR BRUNCH TREAT. THESE SCRAMBLED EGGS ARE SOFTER AND CREAMIER THAN OTHER VERSIONS, AND TASTE GOOD SERVED COLD.

SERVES FOUR

INGREDIENTS
   4 individual brioches
   6 eggs, beaten
   30ml/2 tbsp chopped fresh chives,
     plus extra to serve
   25g/1oz/2 tbsp butter
   45ml/3 tbsp cottage cheese
   60–75ml/4–5 tbsp double
     (heavy) cream
   salt and ground black pepper

COOK'S TIP
If you do not happen to have brioches to hand, these wonderful herbed eggs taste delicious on top of thick slices of toasted bread. Try them piled high on warm focaccia, or on toasted ciabatta, Granary (whole-wheat) bread or English muffins.

1 Preheat the oven to 180°C/350°F/ Gas 4. Cut the tops off the brioches and set aside. Carefully scoop out the centre of each brioche, leaving a bread shell. Put the brioche cases and lids on a baking sheet and bake for 5–6 minutes until hot and crisp.

COOK'S TIP
Save the scooped-out brioche centres and freeze them in an airtight container. Partly thaw and blend or grate them to make crumbs for coating fish or pieces of chicken before frying.

2 Lightly beat the eggs and season to taste. Add about half the chives. Heat the butter in a medium pan until it begins to foam, then add the eggs and cook, stirring with a wooden spoon until semi-solid.

3 Stir in the cottage cheese, cream and the rest of the chives and continue to cook for 1–2 minutes, making sure that the eggs remain soft and creamy.

4 To serve, spoon the eggs into the crisp brioche shells and sprinkle with the extra chives.

BACON, EGG AND CHANTERELLE BAPS

THE DELICATE CHANTERELLE MUSHROOM WITH ITS SLIGHT FRUITINESS COMBINES BEAUTIFULLY WITH EGGS AND BACON FOR THIS RATHER SOPHISTICATED BREAKFAST BAP.

SERVES FOUR

INGREDIENTS

    350g/12oz unsmoked bacon
      rashers (strips)
    50g/2oz/4 tbsp unsalted (sweet)
      butter, plus extra for spreading
    115g/4oz/1½ cups chanterelle
      mushrooms, trimmed and halved
    60ml/4 tbsp sunflower oil
    4 eggs
    4 large baps, split
    salt and ground black pepper

COOK'S TIP
Other varieties of mushroom can be used instead of chanterelles. Try brown cap mushrooms, chestnut mushrooms or, better still, freshly picked field (portabello) mushrooms.

1 Place the bacon in a large non-stick frying pan and fry in its own fat until crisp. Transfer to a heatproof plate, cover and keep warm in a low oven.

2 Melt 25g/1oz/2 tbsp of the butter in the pan, add the chanterelles and fry over a gentle heat until soft, without letting them colour. Transfer to a plate, cover and keep warm.

3 Melt the remaining butter, add the oil and heat to a moderate temperature. Break the eggs into the pan, two at a time, if necessary. Fry them, turning to cook both sides if you like.

4 Toast the baps, spread with butter, then top each with bacon, chanterelles and a fried egg. Season, add the bap lids and serve immediately.

POACHED EGGS FLORENTINE

FLORENTINE DISHES, WHICH ARE COOKED IN "THE STYLE OF FLORENCE", ALWAYS CONTAIN SPINACH AND MAY ALSO BE TOPPED WITH A CREAMY SAUCE.

SERVES FOUR

INGREDIENTS
675g/1½lb spinach, washed
  and drained
25g/1oz/2 tbsp butter
60ml/4 tbsp double (heavy) cream
pinch of freshly grated nutmeg
For the topping
25g/1oz/2 tbsp butter
25g/1oz/¼ cup plain (all-purpose) flour
300ml/½ pint/1¼ cups hot milk
pinch of ground mace
115g/4oz/1 cup grated
  Gruyère cheese
4 eggs
15ml/1 tbsp freshly grated
  Parmesan cheese
salt and ground black pepper

COOK'S TIP
This dish can be prepared with any other green vegetable that is in season, such as chard, fennel or Chinese cabbage.

1 Preheat the oven to 200°C/400°F/ Gas 6. Place the spinach in a large pan with a little water. Cook for 3–4 minutes, then drain well and chop finely. Return to the pan, add the butter, cream, nutmeg and seasoning and heat through. Spoon into four small gratin dishes, making a well in the middle of each.

2 To make the topping, heat the butter in a small pan, add the flour and cook for 1 minute, stirring. Gradually blend in the hot milk, beating well.

3 Cook for 2 minutes, stirring. Remove from the heat and stir in the mace and 75g/3oz/¾ cup of the Gruyère cheese.

4 Break each egg into a cup and slide it into a pan of lightly salted simmering water. Poach for 3–4 minutes. Lift out the eggs using a slotted spoon and drain on kitchen paper. Place a poached egg in the middle of each dish and cover with the cheese sauce. Sprinkle with the remaining cheeses and bake for 10 minutes or until just golden.

OMELETTE ARNOLD BENNETT

CREATED FOR THE AUTHOR, ARNOLD BENNETT, WHO FREQUENTLY DINED AT THE SAVOY HOTEL IN LONDON, THIS CREAMY, SMOKED HADDOCK SOUFFLÉ OMELETTE IS NOW SERVED ALL OVER THE WORLD.

SERVES TWO

INGREDIENTS
 175g/6oz smoked haddock fillet,
  poached and drained
 50g/2oz/4 tbsp butter, diced
 175ml/6fl oz/¾ cup whipping or
  double (heavy) cream
 4 eggs, separated
 40g/1½oz/⅓ cup grated mature
  (sharp) Cheddar cheese
 ground black pepper
 watercress, to garnish

COOK'S TIP
Try to buy smoked haddock that does not contain artificial colouring for this recipe. Besides being better for you, it gives the omelette a lighter, more attractive colour.

1 Remove the skin and any bones from the haddock fillet and discard. Carefully flake the flesh using a fork.

2 Melt half the butter with 60ml/4 tbsp of the cream in a fairly small non-stick pan over a low heat, then add the flaked fish and stir together gently. Cover the pan with a lid, remove from the heat and set aside to cool.

3 Mix the egg yolks with 15ml/1 tbsp of the cream. Season with pepper, then stir into the fish. Mix the cheese and the remaining cream in another bowl. Stiffly whisk the egg whites, then fold into the fish mixture. Heat the remaining butter in an omelette pan, add the fish mixture and cook until browned underneath. Pour the cheese mixture over and grill (broil) until bubbling. Garnish and serve.

STUFFED THAI OMELETTES

THAI FOOD OFTEN CLEVERLY COMBINES HOT CHILLI WITH SWEET FLAVOURS, AS IN THE FILLING FOR THE OMELETTES. IT MAKES AN INTERESTING CONTRAST TO THE DELICATE FLAVOUR OF THE EGG.

SERVES FOUR

INGREDIENTS
  5–6 eggs
  15ml/1 tbsp Thai fish sauce
  30ml/2 tbsp vegetable oil
  sprigs of coriander (cilantro) and red
    chillies, sliced, to garnish
For the filling
  30ml/2 tbsp vegetable oil
  2 garlic cloves, finely chopped
  1 small onion, finely chopped
  225g/8oz/2 cups minced (ground) pork
  30ml/2 tbsp Thai fish sauce
  5ml/1 tsp granulated sugar
  2 tomatoes, peeled and chopped
  15ml/1 tbsp chopped fresh
    coriander (cilantro)
  ground black pepper

1 Heat the oil in a wok, add the garlic and onion and fry for 3–4 minutes until soft. Add the pork and fry for about 8 minutes until lightly browned.

2 Stir in the fish sauce, sugar, tomatoes and pepper; simmer until slightly thickened. Mix in the fresh coriander.

3 To make the omelettes, whisk together the eggs and fish sauce.

4 Heat 15ml/1 tbsp of the oil in an omelette pan or wok. Add half the beaten egg mixture and tilt the pan to spread the egg into a thin, even sheet.

5 Cook until the omelette is just set, then spoon half the filling into the centre. Fold into a neat square parcel by bringing the opposite sides of the omelette towards each other – first the top and bottom, then the right and left sides.

6 Slide the parcel on to a warm serving dish, folded side down. Repeat with the rest of the oil, eggs and filling to make a second omelette parcel. Garnish with sprigs of coriander and red chillies. Cut each omelette in half to serve.

COOK'S TIP
For a milder flavour, discard the seeds and membrane of the chillies where most of their heat resides. Always remember to wash your hands immediately after handling chillies.

OMELETTES FOO YUNG

These unusual breakfast omelettes are served with a traditional Chinese filling.

SERVES FOUR

INGREDIENTS
 15ml/1 tbsp groundnut (peanut) oil
 40g/1½oz/3 tbsp spring onions
   (scallions), chopped
 2 celery sticks
 10ml/2 tsp chopped fresh root ginger
 1 garlic clove, crushed
 40g/1½oz/¼ cup diced cooked ham
 75g/3oz/½ cup crab meat
 75g/3oz/½ cup peeled cooked small
   prawns (shrimp)
 25ml/1½ tbsp chopped fresh
   coriander (cilantro)
 15–30ml/1–2 tbsp soy sauce, plus
   extra for serving
 8–12 eggs, beaten
 80g/3oz/6 tbsp butter
 salt and ground black pepper
 sprigs of coriander (cilantro), to garnish

1 Heat the oil in a large frying pan over a medium heat. Add the spring onions, celery, ginger and garlic and cook for about 1 minute, stirring frequently.

2 Add the ham, crab meat, prawns, fresh coriander and soy sauce. Reduce the heat and leave the mixture to heat through gently, stirring occasionally.

3 To make the omelettes, heat 20g/¾oz/ 1½ tbsp butter in a pan. Season the eggs, add a quarter of the mixture to the pan and cook until it begins to set. Turn over and cook for 2 minutes. Tip on to a serving plate and keep warm. Cook another three omelettes in the same way. Divide the filling among the omelettes and roll up. Serve hot with soy sauce and garnish with coriander.

EGG RICE CAKES WITH MUSHROOMS

The creamy taste and texture of these rice cakes is set off beautifully by the earthy flavour of the wild mushrooms.

SERVES FOUR

INGREDIENTS
 1 egg
 15ml/1 tbsp plain (all-purpose) flour
 60ml/4 tbsp freshly grated Parmesan,
   Fontina or Pecorino cheese
 450g/1lb/2 cups cooked long
   grain rice
 50g/2oz/4 tbsp unsalted (sweet) butter
 30–45ml/2–3 tbsp olive oil
 1 shallot or small onion, chopped
 175g/6oz/1¾ cups assorted wild and
   cultivated mushrooms, such as
   ceps, chanterelles, horn of plenty,
   blewits, field (portabello) and oyster
   mushrooms, trimmed and sliced
 sprig of thyme, plus extra to garnish
 30ml/2 tbsp sherry
 150ml/¼ pint/⅔ cup sour cream
   or crème fraîche
 salt and ground black pepper
 paprika, for dusting (optional)

1 Beat the egg, flour and cheese together with a fork, then stir in the cooked rice. Mix well and set aside.

2 Melt half the butter and oil in a frying pan and sauté the shallot or onion until soft but not brown. Add the mushrooms and thyme and cook until the mushroom juices run. Stir in the sherry. Increase the heat to reduce the juices and concentrate the flavour. Season to taste. Remove from the heat and keep warm.

3 Heat the remaining butter and oil in a large frying pan and fry spoonfuls of the rice mixture in batches. Cook for about 1 minute, then turn over with a spatula and cook for a further 1 minute.

4 When all the rice cakes are cooked, arrange them on one large or four individual warmed plates, with the mushrooms and a spoonful of sour cream or crème fraîche. Garnish with thyme. Dust with paprika if you like.

SOFT TACOS <u>WITH</u> SPICED OMELETTE

SERVED HOT, WARM OR COLD, THESE TACOS MAKE EASY FOOD ON THE MOVE FOR YOUNGER MEMBERS OF THE FAMILY, WHEN THEY NEED SOMETHING NOURISHING TO TAKE ON A PICNIC, HIKE OR BIKE RIDE.

<u>SERVES FOUR</u>

INGREDIENTS
    30ml/2 tbsp sunflower oil
    50g/2oz beansprouts
    50g/2oz carrots, cut into
        thin sticks
    25g/1oz Chinese cabbage, chopped
    15ml/1 tbsp light soy sauce
    4 eggs
    1 small spring onion (scallion),
        thinly sliced
    5ml/1 tsp Cajun seasoning
    25g/1oz/2 tbsp butter
    4 soft flour tortillas, warmed in
        the oven or microwave
    salt and ground black pepper

COOK'S TIP
You can buy fresh soft tortillas in large supermarkets. They freeze well, so keep a packet or two in the freezer.

1 Heat the oil in a small frying pan and stir-fry the beansprouts, carrot sticks and chopped cabbage until they begin to soften. Add the soy sauce, stir to combine and set aside.

2 Place the eggs, sliced spring onion, Cajun seasoning, salt and ground black pepper in a bowl and beat together. Melt the butter in a small pan until it sizzles. Add the beaten eggs and cook over a gentle heat, stirring constantly, until almost firm.

3 Divide the vegetables and scrambled egg evenly among the tortillas, fold up into cones or parcels and serve. For travelling, the tacos can be wrapped in kitchen paper and foil.

VARIATION
Fill warm pitta breads with this spicy omelette mixture. Mini pitta breads are perfect for younger children who may find the folded tacos difficult to handle.

FRENCH COUNTRY-STYLE EGGS

THIS VARIATION ON AN OMELETTE COOKS THE "FILLING" IN THE OMELETTE MIXTURE ITSELF. YOU CAN INCORPORATE LOTS OF DIFFERENT INGREDIENTS, SUCH AS LEFTOVER VEGETABLES.

<u>SERVES TWO</u>

INGREDIENTS
    45–75ml/3–5 tbsp sunflower oil
    50g/2oz thick bacon rashers
        (strips) or pieces, rinds removed
        and chopped
    2 thick slices of bread,
        cut into small cubes
    1 small onion, chopped
    1–2 celery sticks, thinly sliced
    115g/4oz cooked potato, diced
    5 eggs, beaten
    2 garlic cloves, crushed
    handful of young spinach or sorrel
        leaves, stalks removed,
        torn into pieces
    few sprigs of parsley, chopped
    salt and ground black pepper

1 Heat the oil in a large heavy frying pan, and fry the bacon and bread cubes until they are crisp and turning golden. Add the chopped onion, celery and diced potato and continue cooking gently, stirring frequently until all the vegetables are soft and beginning to turn golden brown.

2 Beat the eggs with the garlic and seasoning and pour over the vegetables. When the underside is beginning to set, add the spinach or sorrel. Cook until they have wilted and the omelette is only just soft in the middle. Fold the omelette in half and slide it out of the pan. Serve topped with the parsley.

SPANISH OMELETTE

ALMOST REGARDED AS THE NATIONAL DISH OF SPAIN, THE TRADITIONAL SPANISH OMELETTE CONSISTS SIMPLY OF POTATOES, ONIONS AND EGGS. THIS ONE HAS OTHER VEGETABLES AND WHITE BEANS, TOO, A VARIATION FROM NORTHERN SPAIN, AND MAKES A VERY SUBSTANTIAL VEGETARIAN BRUNCH.

SERVES SIX

INGREDIENTS
    30ml/2 tbsp olive oil, plus extra
      for drizzling
    1 Spanish onion, chopped
    1 red (bell) pepper, seeded and diced
    2 celery sticks, chopped
    225g/8oz potatoes, peeled, diced
      and cooked
    400g/14oz can cannellini
      beans, drained
    8 eggs
    salt and ground black pepper
    sprigs of oregano, to garnish
    green salad and olives, to serve

1 Heat the olive oil in a 30cm/12in frying pan or paella pan. Add the onion, red pepper and celery, and cook for 3–5 minutes until the vegetables are soft, but not coloured.

2 Add the potatoes and beans and cook for several minutes to heat through.

3 In a small bowl, beat the eggs with a fork, then season well and pour over the ingredients in the pan.

4 Stir the egg mixture with a wooden spatula until it begins to thicken, then allow it to cook over a low heat for about 8 minutes. The omelette should be firm, but still moist in the middle. Cool slightly, then invert on to a serving plate.

5 Cut the omelette into thick wedges. Serve warm or cool with a green salad and olives and a little olive oil. Garnish with oregano.

COOK'S TIP
In Spain, this omelette is often served as a tapas dish or appetizer. It is delicious served cold, cut into bitesize pieces and accompanied with a chilli sauce or mayonnaise for dipping. Other sliced seasonal vegetables, baby artichoke hearts and chickpeas can also be used in this recipe.

VEGETABLE PANCAKES <u>WITH</u> TOMATO SALSA

THESE LITTLE SPINACH AND EGG PANCAKES CAN BE PREPARED IN ADVANCE, TO AVOID TOO MUCH LAST-MINUTE COOKING, AND SERVED AS AN UNUSUAL APPETIZER WITH THE SPICY SALSA.

MAKES TEN TO TWELVE

INGREDIENTS
   225g/8oz spinach
   1 small leek
   a few sprigs of fresh parsley
   3 large (US extra large) eggs
   50g/2oz/½ cup plain (all-purpose)
     flour, sifted
   oil, for frying
   25g/1oz/⅓ cup freshly grated
     Parmesan cheese
   salt, ground black pepper and
     grated nutmeg
For the salsa
   2 tomatoes, peeled and chopped
   ¼ fresh red chilli, finely chopped
   2 pieces sun-dried tomato in oil,
     drained and chopped
   1 small red onion, chopped
   1 garlic clove, crushed
   60ml/4 tbsp good olive oil
   30ml/2 tbsp sherry
   2.5ml/½ tsp soft light brown sugar

1 Shred or chop the spinach with the leek and parsley until fine but not puréed. Alternatively, chop them in a food processor, but do not over-process. Beat in the eggs and seasoning to taste. Gradually blend in the flour and 30–45ml/2–3 tbsp water and set aside for 20 minutes.

2 To prepare the tomato salsa, mix together all the ingredients in a bowl, then cover and leave for 2–3 hours for the flavours to infuse (steep).

3 To cook, drop small spoonfuls of the batter into a lightly oiled non-stick frying pan and fry until golden underneath. Turn and cook briefly on the other side. Drain on kitchen paper and keep warm. Sprinkle with Parmesan and serve hot with the spicy tomato salsa.

VARIATION
Use watercress, sorrel or chard or a mixture of sorrel and chard in place of the spinach.

SOUPS AND APPETIZERS

Both the cooking qualities of eggs and their decorative appearance make them the ideal ingredient for tempting soups and appetizers. Eggs can be used to enrich or thicken soups, such as Egg and Cheese Soup, and Avgolemono, and can be used as attractive garnishes in soups, such as Cauliflower Cream Soup and Prawn and Egg-knot Soup. Some cold appetizers, such as Asparagus and Egg Terrine, rely on eggs for setting, and they are ideal for dinner parties because they can be prepared in advance. Delicate and elegant appetizers, such as Quail's Eggs in Aspic with Prosciutto, and Vegetable Tempura, will whet the appetite at the beginning of a meal, while more substantial dishes, such as Twice-baked Soufflés and Leek and Onion Tartlets, will delight guests who have heartier appetites.

CAULIFLOWER CREAM SOUP

THIS DELICATELY FLAVOURED, THICK WINTER SOUP IS ENRICHED AT THE LAST MINUTE WITH CHOPPED EGGS AND CRÈME FRAÎCHE.

SERVES FOUR

INGREDIENTS

  1 cauliflower, cut into large pieces
  1 large onion, roughly chopped
  1 large garlic clove, chopped
  bouquet garni
  5ml/1 tsp ground coriander
  pinch of mustard powder
  900ml/1½ pints/3¾ cups vegetable
    or chicken stock
  5–10ml/1–2 tsp cornflour (cornstarch)
  150ml/¼ pint/⅔ cup milk
  45ml/3 tbsp crème fraîche
  2 eggs, hard-boiled (hard-cooked)
    and roughly chopped
  15ml/1 tbsp chopped fresh
    coriander (cilantro)
  salt and ground black pepper

VARIATION
Use one or two large heads of broccoli in place of the cauliflower.

1 Place the cauliflower in a large pan with the onion, garlic, bouquet garni, coriander, mustard, salt and pepper and stock. Simmer for 10–15 minutes until the cauliflower is tender. Cool slightly.

2 Remove the garlic and bouquet garni, then blend the cauliflower and onion with some of the cooking liquid in a food processor, or press through a sieve for a really smooth result. Return to the pan along with the rest of the liquid.

3 Blend the cornflour with a little of the milk, then add to the soup with the rest of the milk. Return to the heat and cook until thickened, stirring all the time. Season to taste and, just before serving, turn off the heat and blend in the crème fraîche. Stir in the chopped egg and coriander and serve immediately.

COOK'S TIP
Garlic croûtons would make a delicious accompaniment to this smooth soup.

AVGOLEMONO

THE NAME OF THIS POPULAR GREEK SOUP MEANS "EGG AND LEMON", THE TWO KEY INGREDIENTS. IT IS A LIGHT, NOURISHING SOUP MADE WITH ORZO, A GREEK RICE-SHAPED PASTA, BUT YOU CAN USE ANY VERY SMALL PASTA SHAPE IN ITS PLACE.

SERVES FOUR TO SIX

INGREDIENTS

  1.75 litres/3 pints/7½ cups
    chicken stock
  115g/4oz/½ cup orzo pasta
  3 eggs
  juice of 1 large lemon
  salt and ground black pepper
  lemon slices, to garnish

COOK'S TIP
To make your own chicken stock, place a chicken carcass in a large pan with 1 onion, 1 carrot, 1 celery stick, 1 garlic clove and a bouquet garni, cover with water and bring to the boil. Simmer for 2 hours, skimming occasionally. Strain the stock and use as required.

1 Pour the stock into a large pan and bring to the boil. Add the pasta and cook for 5 minutes.

COOK'S TIP
Do not allow the soup to boil once the eggs have been added or they will curdle.

2 Beat the eggs until frothy, then add the lemon juice and 15ml/1 tbsp cold water.

3 Stir in a ladleful of the hot chicken stock, then add 1–2 more. Return this mixture to the pan, remove from the heat and stir well. Season and serve immediately, garnished with lemon.

PRAWN AND EGG-KNOT SOUP

OMELETTES AND PANCAKES ARE OFTEN USED TO ADD PROTEIN TO LIGHT ASIAN SOUPS. IN THIS RECIPE, THIN OMELETTES ARE TWISTED INTO LITTLE KNOTS AND ADDED AT THE LAST MINUTE.

SERVES FOUR

INGREDIENTS
   1 spring onion (scallion), shredded
   800ml/1⅓ pints/3½ cups well-
     flavoured stock or instant dashi
   5ml/1 tsp soy sauce
   dash of sake or dry white wine
   pinch of salt
For the prawn (shrimp) balls
   200g/7oz/generous 1 cup raw large
     prawns (shrimp), peeled
   65g/2½ oz cod fillet, skinned
   5ml/1 tsp egg white
   5ml/1 tsp sake or dry white wine,
     plus a dash extra
   22.5ml/4½ tsp cornflour (cornstarch)
     or potato flour
   2–3 drops soy sauce
   pinch of salt
For the omelette
   1 egg, beaten
   dash of mirin
   pinch of salt
   oil, for cooking

3 To make the omelette, mix the egg with the mirin and salt. Heat a little oil in a frying pan and pour in the egg mixture, coating the pan evenly. When the omelette has set, turn it over and cook for 30 seconds. Leave to cool.

4 Cut the omelette into strips and tie each in a knot. Heat the stock or dashi, then add the soy sauce, sake or wine and salt. Divide the prawn balls and egg-knots among four bowls and add the soup. Garnish with the spring onion.

1 To make the prawn balls, use a pin to remove the black vein running down the back of each prawn. Place the prawns, cod, egg white, sake or dry white wine, cornflour or potato flour, soy sauce and a pinch of salt in a food processor or blender and process to a thick, sticky paste. Shape the mixture into four balls, place in a steaming basket and steam over a pan of vigorously boiling water for about 10 minutes.

2 To make the garnish, soak the spring onion in iced water for about 5 minutes, until it curls, then drain.

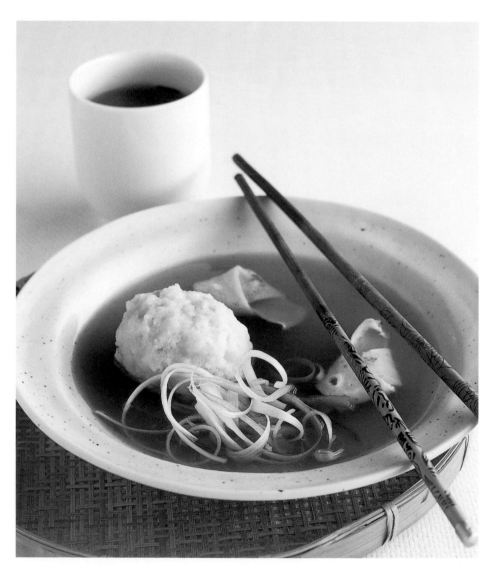

EGG AND CHEESE SOUP

IN THIS CLASSIC ROMAN SOUP, EGGS AND CHEESE ARE BEATEN INTO HOT SOUP, PRODUCING THE SLIGHTLY SCRAMBLED TEXTURE THAT IS CHARACTERISTIC OF THIS DISH.

SERVES SIX

INGREDIENTS
   3 eggs
   45ml/3 tbsp fine semolina
   90ml/6 tbsp freshly grated
     Parmesan cheese
   pinch of grated nutmeg
   1.5 litres/2½ pints/6¼ cups cold
     meat or chicken stock
   salt and ground black pepper
   12 rounds of country bread or
     ciabatta, to serve

COOK'S TIP
Once added to the hot soup, the egg will begin to cook and the soup will become less smooth. Try not to overcook the soup at this stage because it may cause the egg to curdle.

1 Beat the eggs in a bowl, then beat in the semolina and the cheese. Add the nutmeg and beat in 250ml/8fl oz/ 1 cup of the meat or chicken stock. Pour the mixture into a jug (pitcher).

2 Pour the remaining stock into a large pan and bring to a gentle simmer.

3 A few minutes before you are ready to serve the soup, whisk the egg mixture into the hot stock. Raise the heat slightly, and bring it barely to the boil. Season and cook for 3–4 minutes.

4 To serve, toast the rounds of country bread or ciabatta until golden, place two in each soup plate and ladle on the hot soup. Serve immediately.

QUAIL'S EGGS IN ASPIC WITH PROSCIUTTO

THESE PRETTY LITTLE EGGS IN JELLY ARE SO EASY TO MAKE, AND ARE GREAT FOR SUMMER DINING.
THEY ARE EXCELLENT SERVED WITH A SALAD AND HOME-MADE MAYONNAISE.

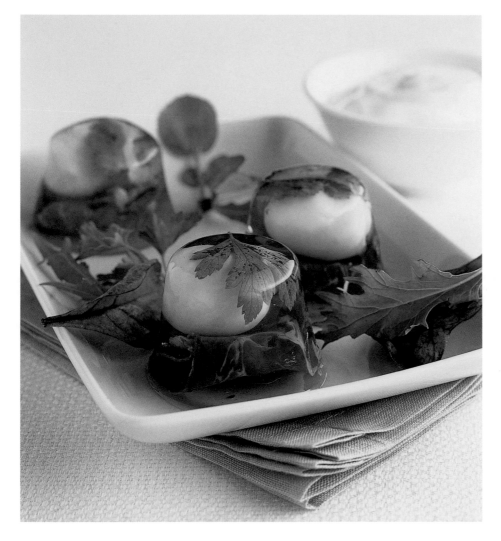

2 Meanwhile, put the quail's eggs in a pan of cold water and bring to the boil. Boil for 1½ minutes, then pour off the hot water and leave in cold water until completely cool. This way the yolks should still be a little soft but the eggs will be firm enough to peel.

3 Rinse 12 dariole moulds but do not dry, then place the moulds on a tray. Cut each slice of ham in half and roll or fold so that they will fit into the moulds.

4 Place a coriander or parsley leaf flat in the base of each mould, then put a peeled egg on top. As the jelly begins to thicken, spoon in enough to nearly cover each egg, holding the egg steady. Put a slice of ham on each egg and pour in the rest of the jelly to fill the moulds.

MAKES TWELVE

INGREDIENTS
   22g/¾oz packet aspic powder
   45ml/3 tbsp dry sherry
   12 quail's eggs or other small eggs
   6 slices of prosciutto
   12 fresh coriander (cilantro) or flat
      leaf parsley leaves

COOK'S TIP
Instead of dariole moulds, use small ramekins. When using larger moulds, use proportionally larger eggs as well, such as bantam, pheasant, guinea fowl or very small hen's eggs, so that the finished moulds don't have too much aspic jelly. One packet of aspic should make enough jelly to fill 8–9 small ramekins.

1 To make the aspic jelly, follow the instructions on the packet, but replace 45ml/3 tbsp of the recommended quantity of water with the dry sherry to give a greater depth of flavour. Leave the aspic jelly in the refrigerator until it begins to thicken, but do not let it become too thick or nearly set.

5 Transfer the tray of moulds to a cool place and leave for 3–4 hours until set and cold. When ready to serve, run a knife around the sides of the jelly to loosen. Dip the moulds into warm water and tap gently until they become loose. Invert the eggs on to small plates and serve with salad.

ASPARAGUS AND EGG TERRINE

FOR LIGHT SUMMER EATING OR A SPECIAL DINNER, THIS TERRINE IS DELICIOUS YET VERY AIRY. MAKE THE HOLLANDAISE SAUCE WELL IN ADVANCE AND WARM THROUGH GENTLY WHEN REQUIRED.

SERVES EIGHT

INGREDIENTS
    150ml/¼ pint/⅔ cup milk
    150ml/¼ pint/⅔ cup double
      (heavy) cream
    40g/1½oz/3 tbsp butter
    40g/1½oz/⅓ cup flour
    75g/3oz/generous ⅓ cup herb or
      garlic cream cheese
    675g/1½lb asparagus spears, cooked
    a little oil
    2 eggs, separated
    15ml/1 tbsp chopped fresh chives
    30ml/2 tbsp chopped fresh dill
    salt and ground black pepper
    sprigs of fresh dill, to garnish
    mixed salad leaves, to serve
For the sauce
    15ml/1 tbsp white wine vinegar
    15ml/1 tbsp fresh orange juice
    4 black peppercorns
    1 bay leaf
    2 egg yolks
    115g/4oz/½ cup butter, melted

1 Put the milk and cream into a small pan and heat to just below boiling point. Melt the butter in a pan, stir in the flour and cook for 1 minute. Gradually whisk in the milk and cream and cook for about 1–2 minutes to make a very thick sauce. Stir in the cream cheese, season and leave to cool.

2 Trim the cooked asparagus spears to fit the width of a 1.3 litre/2¼ pint/5⅔ cup loaf tin (pan) or terrine. Lightly oil the tin and line the base with a piece of greaseproof (waxed) paper. Preheat the oven to 180°C/350°F/Gas 4.

3 Beat the yolks into the sauce mixture. In a separate bowl, whisk the whites until stiff then fold into the sauce mixture with the chives, dill and seasoning. Layer the asparagus and egg mixture in the tin, starting and finishing with asparagus. Cover the top with foil. Place the terrine in a roasting pan half-filled with water and bake for about 50 minutes until just firm to the touch.

4 To make the sauce, put the vinegar, orange juice, peppercorns and bay leaf in a small pan and cook for 2 minutes, or until reduced by at least half. Leave to cool slightly.

5 Whisk the egg yolks into the vinegar and orange mixture using a balloon whisk. Place the pan over a gentle heat and whisk in the butter. Season to taste and keep whisking until glossy and thick. Leave to cool, then reheat over a pan of hot water when ready to serve.

6 When the terrine is just firm to the touch remove from the oven and allow to cool, then chill. To serve, carefully invert the terrine on to a serving dish, remove the greaseproof paper and garnish with sprigs of dill. Serve cut into slices with the warm sauce.

STILTON CROQUETTES

THESE ARE PERFECT LITTLE PARTY BITES, WHICH YOU CAN MAKE IN ADVANCE AND REHEAT AT THE LAST MINUTE. FOR A REALLY CRISP RESULT, DOUBLE COAT THE CROQUETTES IN BREADCRUMBS.

MAKES ABOUT TWENTY

INGREDIENTS

350g/12oz floury potatoes, cooked
75g/3oz creamy Stilton, crumbled
3 eggs, hard-boiled (hard-cooked),
  peeled and chopped
few drops of Worcestershire sauce
a little plain (all-purpose) flour
1 egg, beaten
45–60ml/3–4 tbsp fine breadcrumbs
vegetable oil, for deep-frying
salt and ground black pepper
dipping sauce, to serve

COOK'S TIP
You can make these croquettes in advance and freeze them before frying. To thaw, leave them to stand in a warm place for 1 hour before frying.

1 Mash the potatoes until quite smooth. Work in the crumbled Stilton cheese, chopped egg and Worcestershire sauce. Add seasoning to taste.

2 Divide the potato and cheese mixture into about 20 pieces and shape into small sausage or cork shapes, no longer than 2.5cm/1in.

3 Coat in flour, then dip into the beaten egg and coat evenly in breadcrumbs. Reshape, if necessary. Chill for about 30 minutes then deep-fry, 7–8 at a time, in hot oil turning frequently until they are golden brown all over. Drain on kitchen paper, transfer to a serving dish and keep warm for up to 30 minutes. Serve with a dipping sauce.

VEGETABLE TEMPURA

TEMPURA ARE JAPANESE SAVOURY FRITTERS. THEY ARE TRADITIONALLY MADE WITH PRAWNS, BUT MONKFISH AND VEGETABLES CAN ALSO BE USED. THE SECRET OF MAKING THE INCREDIBLY LIGHT BATTER IS TO USE REALLY COLD WATER, AND TO HAVE THE OIL FOR FRYING AT THE RIGHT TEMPERATURE.

SERVES FOUR

INGREDIENTS
  2 courgettes (zucchini)
  ½ aubergine (eggplant)
  1 large carrot
  ½ small Spanish onion
  1 egg
  120ml/4fl oz/½ cup iced water
  115g/4oz/1 cup plain (all-
    purpose) flour
  vegetable oil, for deep-frying
  salt and ground black pepper
  sea salt flakes, lemon slices and
    Japanese soy sauce (shoyu),
    to serve

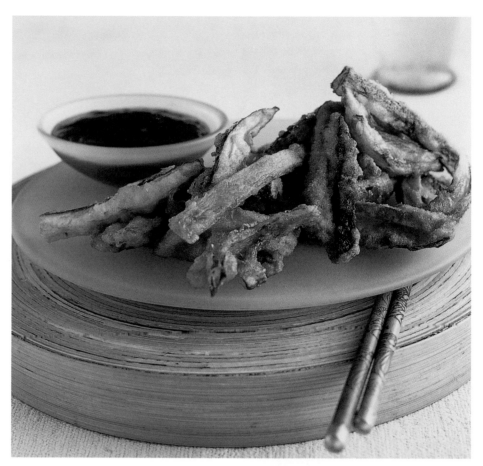

1 Using a vegetable peeler, pare strips of peel from the courgettes and aubergine.

2 Using a large, sharp knife, cut the courgettes, aubergine and carrot into strips about 7.5–10cm/3–4in long and 6mm/¼in wide.

3 Put the courgettes, aubergine and carrot strips into a colander and sprinkle liberally with salt. Put a small plate over the vegetables, weight it down and leave for about 30 minutes, then rinse thoroughly under cold running water. Drain thoroughly, then dry the vegetables with kitchen paper.

4 Thinly slice the onion from top to bottom, discarding the plump pieces in the middle. Separate the layers so that there are lots of fine, long strips. Mix all the vegetables together and season with salt and pepper.

5 Make the batter immediately before frying. Mix the egg and iced water in a bowl, then sift in the flour. Mix briefly with a fork or chopsticks. Do not overmix; the batter should remain lumpy. Add the vegetables to the batter and mix to coat.

VARIATION
Other suitable vegetables for tempura include mushrooms and (bell) peppers.

6 Half-fill a wok with oil and heat to 180°C/350°F. Scoop up 1 heaped tablespoon of the mixture at a time and carefully lower it into the oil. Deep-fry in batches for about 3 minutes until golden brown and crisp. Drain on kitchen paper.

7 Serve each portion with salt, slices of lemon and a tiny bowl of Japanese soy sauce for dipping.

STEAMED THAI EGGS WITH PRAWNS

THIS GENTLY COOKED EGG DISH CONTAINS A SURPRISING KICK OF CHILLI, GINGER AND GARLIC. BE SURE YOU HAVE A STEAMER, COLANDER OR SIEVE WITH A TIGHT-FITTING LID OTHERWISE THE EGGS WILL TAKE MUCH LONGER TO COOK.

SERVES FOUR

INGREDIENTS
  a little oil
  175g/6oz/1 cup peeled
    prawns (shrimp)
  5ml/1 tsp grated fresh root ginger
  5ml/1 tsp fish sauce
  1 large garlic clove, thinly sliced
  15–30ml/1–2 tbsp soy sauce
  2 large spring onions (scallions),
    thinly sliced
  4 eggs
  50ml/2fl oz/¼ cup vegetable stock
  5ml/1 tsp sesame oil
  5ml/1 tsp very finely chopped fresh
    red chilli, plus extra to garnish
  salt and ground black pepper
  shredded Chinese cabbage and thinly
    sliced cucumber, to serve (optional)

1 Lightly oil four large ramekin dishes. Put the prawns in a large bowl and stir in the ginger, fish sauce, garlic, soy sauce and half the spring onions.

COOK'S TIP
If the steamer does not have a tightly fitting lid, cook for a few more minutes to ensure the eggs are cooked through.

2 Put the eggs into another bowl, whisk in the stock, oil and chilli, without letting the eggs get too frothy. Add the prawn mixture and divide among the ramekins.

3 Place the ramekins in a steamer over a pan of simmering water, cover and cook for 15 minutes until set. Remove from the heat and leave to cool.

EGGS IN RED WINE

THIS IS A VARIATION ON A CLASSIC FRENCH RECIPE OEUFS EN MEURETTE BUT IS MUCH LIGHTER AND LESS RICH. TRADITIONALLY, THE EGGS ARE POACHED IN THE WINE RATHER THAN WATER.

SERVES SIX

INGREDIENTS
  40g/1½oz/3 tbsp butter
  150g/5oz streaky (fatty) bacon, rinds
    removed, and roughly chopped
  1 large onion, chopped
  2 shallots, chopped
  1 large garlic clove, chopped
  750ml/1¼ pints/3 cups red wine
  1 clove
  5ml/1 tsp sugar
  1 bay leaf
  1 sprig fresh thyme or
    5ml/1 tsp dried
  25g/1oz/¼ cup plain (all-purpose) flour
  6 slices of French bread
  15g/½oz/1 tbsp butter, softened
    or melted
  6 eggs
  salt and ground black pepper
  sprigs of thyme, to garnish

1 Melt half the butter in a pan and fry the bacon gently for 5 minutes. Then add the onion, shallots and garlic, and cook, stirring, for a further 5 minutes.

2 Add the wine, clove, sugar and herbs and simmer for about 15 minutes to reduce by about one-third.

3 Leave the sauce to cool until you can pick out the bacon to reserve. Remove the bay leaf, thyme and clove, then sieve the sauce or purée in a blender.

4 Melt the rest of the butter in a pan and stir in the flour to make a roux. On a very low heat, gradually whisk in the wine purée and cook for 2–3 minutes until thickened, whisking all the time. Add 30–45ml/2–3 tbsp water to give a lighter consistency and whisk well. Return the bacon to the sauce.

5 Meanwhile, brush the bread on both sides with the soft or melted butter and grill (broil) until golden on both sides.

6 Break the eggs, two at a time, into cups and slide into a pan of gently simmering water. Poach for 3 minutes, then remove and drain well on kitchen paper. To serve, spoon a little sauce on to the toast, top with the eggs and garnish with thyme.

LEEK <u>AND</u> ONION TARTLETS

*THESE ATTRACTIVE LITTLE TARTLETS MAKE A WONDERFUL APPETIZER AND ARE PERFECT FOR BUFFETS.
SMALLER VERSIONS CAN ALSO BE MADE AND MAKE FABULOUS PARTY FOOD.*

SERVES SIX

INGREDIENTS
  25g/1oz/2 tbsp butter, plus extra
    for greasing
  1 onion, thinly sliced
  2.5ml/½ tsp dried thyme
  450g/1lb/4 cups leeks, thinly sliced
  50g/2oz/½ cup grated Gruyère cheese
  3 eggs
  300ml/½ pint/1¼ cups single (light)
    cream
  pinch of freshly grated nutmeg
  salt and ground black pepper
  mixed salad leaves, to serve
For the pastry
  175g/6oz/1½ cups plain (all-
    purpose) flour
  75g/3oz/6 tbsp cold butter
  1 egg yolk
  30–45ml/2–3 tbsp cold water
  2.5ml/½ tsp salt

1 To make the pastry, sift the flour into a large bowl. Rub in the butter with your fingertips until the mixture resembles fine breadcrumbs.

2 Make a well in the flour mixture. Beat together the egg yolk, water and salt. Pour into the well and mix lightly to form a stiff dough. Form into a flattened ball. Wrap and chill for 30 minutes.

3 Butter six 10cm/4in tartlet tins (muffin pans). Roll out the dough on a floured surface to 3mm/⅛in thick. Cut out rounds with a 12.5cm/5in cutter. Ease the rounds into the tins, pressing into the base and sides. Reroll the trimmings and line the remaining tins. Prick the bases and chill for 30 minutes.

4 Preheat the oven to 190°C/375°F/Gas 5. Line the pastry cases with foil and fill with baking beans. Place them on a baking sheet and bake for 6–8 minutes until golden at the edges. Remove the foil and beans, and bake for 2 minutes until the bases appear dry. Transfer to a wire rack to cool. Reduce the oven temperature to 180°C/350°F/Gas 4.

5 In a large frying pan, melt the butter over a medium heat, then add the onion and thyme and cook for 3–5 minutes until the onion is just softened, stirring frequently. Add the leeks and cook for 10–12 minutes until they are soft and tender. Divide the mixture among the pastry cases and sprinkle each with cheese, dividing it evenly.

6 In a medium bowl, beat the eggs, cream, nutmeg and salt and pepper. Place the pastry cases on a baking sheet and pour on the egg mixture. Bake for 15–20 minutes until set and golden. Transfer the tartlets to a wire rack to cool slightly, then remove them from the tins and serve warm or at room temperature with salad leaves.

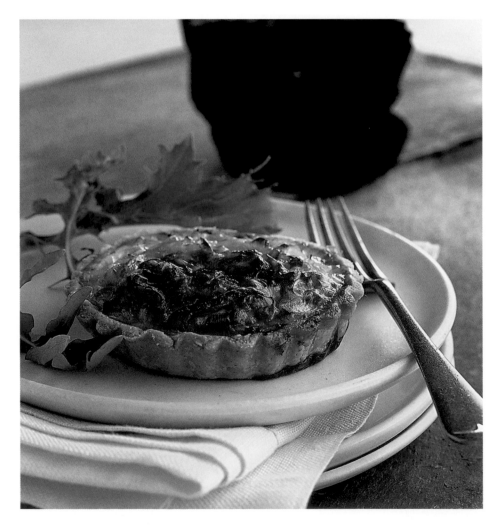

EGG AND SALMON PUFF PARCELS

THESE ELEGANT PARCELS HIDE A MOUTHWATERING COLLECTION OF FLAVOURS, AND MAKE A DELICIOUS APPETIZER OR LUNCH DISH. SERVE WITH CURRY-FLAVOURED MAYONNAISE OR HOLLANDAISE SAUCE.

SERVES SIX

INGREDIENTS
    75g/3oz/scant ½ cup long grain rice
    300ml/½ pint/1¼ cups fish stock
    350g/12oz tail piece of salmon
    juice of ½ lemon
    15ml/1 tbsp chopped fresh dill
    15ml/1 tbsp chopped fresh parsley
    10ml/2 tsp mild curry powder
    6 small (US medium) eggs, soft-
      boiled (soft-cooked) and cooled
    425g/15oz flaky or puff pastry
    1 small egg, beaten
    salt and ground black pepper

1 Cook the rice in the fish stock according to the packet instructions, then drain and set aside to cool. Preheat the oven to 220°C/425°F/Gas 7.

2 Place the salmon in a large pan and cover with cold water. Gently heat until almost simmering and cook for about 8 minutes until it flakes easily. Lift the salmon out of the pan with a fish slice (spatula). Remove the bones and skin. Flake the fish into the rice, add the lemon juice, herbs, curry powder and seasoning and mix well. Peel the eggs.

3 Roll out the pastry and cut into six 14–15cm/5½–6in squares. Brush the edges with the beaten egg. Place a spoonful of the rice mixture in the middle of each square, push a boiled egg into the centre and top with a little more of the rice mixture. Pull over the pastry corners to the middle to form a square parcel, pressing the joins together firmly to seal.

4 Brush the parcels with more beaten egg, place on a baking sheet and bake for 20 minutes, then reduce the oven temperature to 190°C/375°F/Gas 5 and cook for a further 10 minutes or until golden and crisp underneath. Cool slightly before serving.

TWICE-BAKED SOUFFLÉS

THESE LITTLE SOUFFLÉS ARE SERVED UPSIDE DOWN. THEY ARE REMARKABLY SIMPLE TO MAKE AND CAN BE PREPARED UP TO A DAY IN ADVANCE, THEN REHEATED IN THE SAUCE JUST BEFORE SERVING. THEY ARE PERFECT FOR EASY, STRESS-FREE ENTERTAINING.

SERVES SIX

INGREDIENTS
  20g/¾ oz/1½ tbsp butter
  30ml/2 tbsp plain (all-purpose) flour
  150ml/¼ pint/⅔ cup milk
  1 small bay leaf
  2 eggs, separated, plus 1 egg white
  115g/4oz/1 cup grated Gruyère cheese
  1.5ml/¼ tsp cream of tartar
  250ml/8fl oz/1 cup double
    (heavy) cream
  25g/1oz/¼ cup flaked (sliced) almonds
  salt, ground black pepper and
    grated nutmeg
  sprigs of parsley, to garnish

1 Preheat the oven to 190°C/375°F/Gas 5. Lightly grease six 175ml/6fl oz/¾ cup ramekins. Line the bases with buttered greaseproof (waxed) paper.

2 In a small pan, melt the butter over a medium heat, stir in the flour and cook for 1 minute, stirring. Whisk in half the milk until smooth, then whisk in the remaining milk. Add the bay leaf and seasoning. Bring to the boil and cook, stirring constantly, for 1 minute.

3 Remove the pan from the heat and discard the bay leaf. Beat the egg yolks, one at a time, into the hot sauce, then stir in the cheese until it is completely melted. Set aside.

4 In a large, clean, grease-free bowl, whisk the egg whites slowly until they become frothy. Add the cream of tartar, then increase the speed and whisk until they form soft peaks that just flop over at the top.

5 Whisk a spoonful of beaten egg whites into the cheese sauce to lighten it. Pour the cheese sauce over the remaining whites. Using a rubber spatula or large metal spoon, gently fold the sauce into the whites, cutting down through the centre to the bottom, then along the side of the bowl and up to the top.

VARIATION
Other strong cheeses could be used in place of the Gruyère. Try mature (sharp) Cheddar, blue Stilton, Emmenthal or farmhouse Lancashire cheese.

6 Spoon the soufflé mixture into the prepared ramekins, filling them about three-quarters full. Put the ramekins in a shallow ovenproof dish and pour in boiling water to come halfway up their sides. Bake for about 18 minutes until puffed and golden brown. Let the soufflés cool in the ramekins just long enough for them to deflate.

7 Increase the oven temperature to 220°C/425°F/Gas 7. Run a knife around the edge of the soufflés and invert on to an ovenproof dish or individual dishes. Remove the lining paper.

8 Lightly season the cream and pour over the soufflés, sprinkle with almonds and bake for 10–15 minutes until well risen and golden. Serve immediately, garnished with sprigs of parsley.

COOK'S TIP
If you are making these soufflés in advance, cool the once-cooked soufflés, then cover and chill. It is important to bring the soufflés back to room temperature before baking, so remove them from the refrigerator in good time.

LUNCHES AND
LIGHT SUPPERS

Eggs can be combined with other ingredients to create all sorts of quick and delicious light meals. Poached or boiled eggs or strips of omelette can be added to mixed salad leaves or wholesome grains to make a perfect lunch or supper. Alternatively, eggs can be used to fill pastries, such as Cheese and Onion Flan or Egg and Spinach Pie, or to top pizzas, such as Fiorentina Pizza. They can also be used to make wonderful batter dishes, such as Baked Mediterranean Vegetables and Baked Herb Crêpes, which are delicious for a light but warming supper. All the dishes in this chapter are either quick and easy to make or can be prepared in advance, making them ideal for speedy weekday lunches and suppers.

EGG AND FENNEL TABBOULEH WITH NUTS

TABBOULEH IS A MIDDLE EASTERN SALAD OF STEAMED BULGUR WHEAT, FLAVOURED WITH LOTS OF PARSLEY, MINT, LEMON JUICE AND GARLIC. IT IS PERFECT AT A SUMMER BARBECUE.

SERVES FOUR

INGREDIENTS

250g/9oz/1¼ cups bulgur wheat
4 small (US medium) eggs
1 fennel bulb
1 bunch of spring onions
  (scallions), chopped
25g/1oz/½ cup drained sun-dried
  tomatoes in oil, sliced
45ml/3 tbsp chopped fresh parsley
30ml/2 tbsp chopped fresh mint
75g/3oz/½ cup black olives
60ml/4 tbsp olive oil, preferably
  Greek or Spanish
30ml/2 tbsp garlic oil
30ml/2 tbsp lemon juice
50g/2oz/½ cup chopped
  hazelnuts, toasted
1 open-textured loaf or
  4 pitta breads, warmed
salt and ground black pepper

1 Put the bulgur wheat into a bowl. Pour over boiling water and leave to soak for about 15 minutes.

2 Drain the bulgur wheat in a metal sieve and place the sieve over a pan of boiling water. Cover the pan and sieve with a lid and steam for 10 minutes. Fluff up the grains with a fork and spread them out on a metal tray. Set aside to cool.

3 Hard-boil (hard-cook) the eggs for 8 minutes. Cool under running water, peel and quarter, or, using an egg slicer, slice not quite all the way through.

4 Halve and thinly slice the fennel. Boil in salted water for 6 minutes, drain and cool under running water.

5 Combine the eggs, fennel, spring onions, sun-dried tomatoes, parsley, mint and olives with the bulgur wheat. Dress with olive oil, garlic oil and lemon juice and sprinkle with hazelnuts. Season well and serve with bread.

COOK'S TIP

If you are short of time, simply soak the bulgur wheat in boiling water for about 20 minutes until the grains are tender. Drain and rinse under cold water to cool, then drain thoroughly.

WARM DRESSED SALAD WITH POACHED EGGS

SOFT POACHED EGGS, CHILLI, HOT CROÛTONS AND COOL, CRISP SALAD LEAVES MAKE A LIVELY AND UNUSUAL COMBINATION. THIS DELICIOUS SALAD IS PERFECT FOR A SUMMER LUNCH.

SERVES TWO

INGREDIENTS
 ½ small Granary (whole-wheat) loaf
 45ml/3 tbsp chilli oil
 2 eggs
 115g/4oz mixed salad leaves
 45ml/3 tbsp extra virgin olive oil
 2 garlic cloves, crushed
 15ml/1 tbsp balsamic or
  sherry vinegar
 50g/2oz Parmesan cheese, shaved
 ground black pepper (optional)

1 Carefully cut the crust from the Granary loaf and discard. Cut the bread into 2.5cm/1in cubes.

2 Heat the chilli oil in a large frying pan. Add the bread cubes and cook for about 5 minutes, tossing the cubes occasionally, until they are crisp and golden brown all over.

COOK'S TIP
If you are very sensitive to spicy flavours, cook the croûtons in olive oil or a nut oil, such as walnut or hazelnut, rather than using chilli oil.

3 Meanwhile, bring a pan of water to the boil. Break each egg into a jug (pitcher) and carefully slide into the water, one at a time. Gently poach for about 4 minutes until lightly cooked.

4 Divide the salad leaves among two plates. Remove the croûtons from the pan and arrange them over the leaves.

5 Wipe the pan clean with kitchen paper. Then heat the olive oil in the pan, add the garlic and vinegar and cook over high heat for 1 minute. Pour the warm dressing over the salads.

6 Place a poached egg on each salad. Top with thin Parmesan shavings and a little black pepper, if you like.

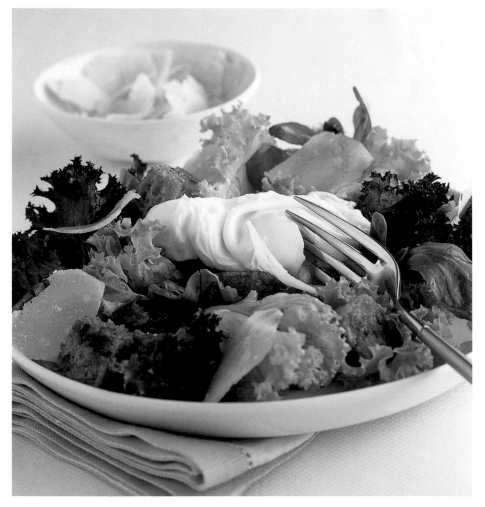

SALAD WITH OMELETTE STRIPS AND BACON

RICH DUCK EGGS ARE DELICIOUS IN SALADS AND, WHEN COOKED AS AN OMELETTE, THEY HAVE A LOVELY, DELICATE FLAVOUR.

SERVES FOUR

INGREDIENTS
    400g/14oz bag of mixed salad leaves
    6 streaky (fatty) bacon rashers
        (strips), rinds removed and chopped
    2 duck eggs
    2 spring onions (scallions), chopped
    few sprigs of coriander
        (cilantro), chopped
    25g/1oz/2 tbsp butter
    60ml/4 tbsp olive oil
    30ml/2 tbsp balsamic vinegar
    salt and ground black pepper

COOK'S TIP
Choose salad leaves that include some distinctively flavoured leaves which will add a bite to this salad. A combination that includes rocket (arugula), watercress or herbs would be ideal.

1 Warm an omelette pan over a low heat and gently fry the chopped bacon until the fat runs. Increase the heat to crisp up the bacon, stirring frequently. When the bacon pieces are brown and crispy, remove from the heat and transfer to a hot dish to keep warm.

2 Beat the eggs with the spring onions and coriander and season.

3 Melt the butter in an omelette pan and pour in the beaten eggs. Cook for 2–3 minutes to make an unfolded omelette. Cut into long strips and add to the salad with the bacon.

4 Place the salad leaves in a large bowl. Add the oil, vinegar and seasoning to the omelette pan, heat briefly and pour over the salad. Toss well before serving.

CHILLI SALAD OMELETTES WITH HUMMUS

THESE DELICATE OMELETTES ARE FILLED WITH SALAD AND SERVED CHILLED, MAKING A REFRESHING LUNCH.

SERVES SIX

INGREDIENTS
    4 eggs
    15ml/1 tbsp cornflour (cornstarch)
    15ml/1 tbsp stock or water
    115g/4oz/1 cup shredded salad
        vegetables, such as crisp lettuce,
        carrot, celery, spring onion
        (scallion) and (bell) peppers
    60ml/4 tbsp chilli salad dressing (or
        add a few drops of chilli sauce to
        your favourite salad dressing)
    60–75ml/4–5 tbsp hummus
    4 crisply cooked bacon rashers
        (strips), chopped
    salt and ground black pepper

VARIATIONS
These omelettes can be filled with a whole range of ingredients. Try using taramasalata instead of hummus, or fill the omelettes with ratatouille.

1 Break the eggs into a bowl. Add the cornflour and stock or water and beat well. Heat a lightly oiled frying pan and pour a quarter of the egg mixture into the pan, tipping it to spread it out to a thin, even layer. Cook the omelette gently to avoid it colouring too much or becoming bubbly and crisp. When cooked, remove from the pan and make a further three omelettes in the same way. Stack them between sheets of baking parchment, then cool and chill.

2 When ready to serve, toss the shredded salad vegetables together with 45ml/3 tbsp of the dressing. Spread half of each omelette with hummus, top with the salad vegetables and chopped bacon and fold in half. Drizzle the rest of the dressing over the filled omelettes before serving.

COOK'S TIP
These wafer-thin omelettes can be made in advance and stored in the refrigerator.

BAKED MEDITERRANEAN VEGETABLES

CRUNCHY GOLDEN BATTER SURROUNDS THESE VEGETABLES, MAKING THEM DELICIOUS AND FILLING. SERVE WITH SALAD AS A LIGHT LUNCH, OR SAUSAGES FOR A MORE SUBSTANTIAL MEAL.

SERVES SIX

INGREDIENTS
  1 small aubergine (eggplant),
    trimmed, halved and thickly sliced
  1 egg
  115g/4oz/1 cup plain (all-
    purpose) flour
  300ml/½ pint/1¼ cups milk
  30ml/2 tbsp fresh thyme leaves
  1 red onion
  2 large courgettes (zucchini)
  1 red (bell) pepper
  1 yellow (bell) pepper
  60–75ml/4–5 tbsp sunflower oil
  30ml/2 tbsp freshly grated
    Parmesan cheese
  salt and ground black pepper
  fresh herbs, to serve

1 Place the aubergine in a colander or sieve, sprinkle generously with salt and leave for 10 minutes. Drain, rinse well and pat dry on kitchen paper.

2 Meanwhile, beat the egg in a bowl, then gradually beat in the flour and a little milk to make a smooth thick paste. Gradually blend in the rest of the milk, add the thyme leaves and seasoning to taste and stir until smooth. Leave the batter in a cool place until required. Preheat the oven to 220°C/425°F/Gas 7.

COOK'S TIP
As with Yorkshire pudding, it is essential to get the oil in the dish really hot before adding the batter, which should sizzle slightly as it goes in. If the fat is not hot enough, the batter will not rise well. Use a pan that is not too deep.

3 Quarter the onion, slice the courgettes and seed and quarter the peppers. Put the oil in a roasting pan and heat in the oven at 220°C/425°F/Gas 7. Add the prepared vegetables, toss in the oil to coat thoroughly and return to the oven for 20 minutes.

4 Give the batter another whisk, then pour it over the vegetables and return the pan to the oven for 30 minutes. When puffed up and golden, reduce the heat to 190°C/375°F/Gas 5 for 10–15 minutes until crisp around the edges. Sprinkle with Parmesan and herbs and serve.

FIORENTINA PIZZA

AN EGG ADDS THE FINISHING TOUCH TO THIS SPINACH PIZZA; TRY NOT TO OVERCOOK IT THOUGH, AS IT'S BEST WHEN THE YOLK IS STILL SLIGHTLY SOFT IN THE MIDDLE.

SERVES TWO TO THREE

INGREDIENTS
45ml/3 tbsp olive oil
1 small red onion, thinly sliced
175g/6oz fresh spinach,
  stalks removed
1 pizza base, about
  25–30cm/10–12in in diameter
1 small jar pizza sauce
freshly grated nutmeg
150g/5oz mozzarella cheese
1 egg
25g/1oz/¼ cup grated Gruyère cheese

1 Heat 15ml/1 tbsp of the oil and fry the onion until soft. Add the spinach and fry until wilted. Drain any excess liquid.

2 Preheat the oven to 220°C/425°F/Gas 7. Brush the pizza base with half the remaining olive oil. Spread the pizza sauce evenly over the base, using the back of a spoon, then top with the spinach mixture. Sprinkle over a little freshly grated nutmeg.

3 Thinly slice the mozzarella and arrange over the spinach. Drizzle over the remaining oil. Bake for 10 minutes, then remove from the oven.

4 Make a small well in the centre of the pizza topping and carefully break the egg into the hole.

5 Sprinkle over the grated Gruyère cheese and return to the oven for a further 5–10 minutes until crisp and golden. Serve immediately.

VARIATION
Italians make a folded pizza called calzone. It is made in the same way as a pizza, but is folded in half to conceal the filling. Add the egg with the rest of the pizza topping, fold over the dough, seal the edges and bake for 20 minutes.

CHEESE AND ONION FLAN

THE USE OF YEAST DOUGHS FOR TARTS AND FLANS IS POPULAR IN VARIOUS REGIONS OF FRANCE.
CHOOSE A STRONG CHEESE SUCH AS LIVAROT, MUNSTER OR PORT SALUT IN THIS RECIPE.

SERVES FOUR

INGREDIENTS
    15g/½oz/1 tbsp butter
    1 onion, halved and sliced
    2 eggs
    250ml/8fl oz/1 cup single
      (light) cream
    225g/8oz strong semi-soft cheese,
      rind removed, sliced
    salt and ground black pepper
    salad leaves, to serve
For the yeast dough
    10ml/2 tsp dried yeast
    120ml/4fl oz/½ cup milk
    5ml/1 tsp sugar
    1 egg yolk
    225g/8oz/2 cups plain (all-purpose)
      flour, plus extra for kneading
    2.5ml/½ tsp salt
    50g/2oz/4 tbsp butter, softened

1 To make the dough, place the yeast in a bowl. Warm the milk in a small pan until it is lukewarm and then stir into the yeast with the sugar. Continue stirring until the yeast has dissolved completely. Leave the yeast mixture to stand for about 3 minutes, then beat in the egg yolk.

COOK'S TIP
If you prefer to use easy-blend (rapid-rise) dried yeast, omit step 1. Beat the egg yolk and milk together in a jug (pitcher). Add the yeast to the flour and salt in a food processor and pulse to combine. Pour in the egg and milk mixture, and proceed with the recipe.

2 Put the flour and salt in a food processor fitted with a metal blade and pulse to combine. With the machine running, slowly pour in the yeast mixture. Scrape down the sides and continue processing for 2–3 minutes. Add the softened butter and process for another 30 seconds.

3 Transfer the dough to a lightly greased bowl. Cover the bowl with a dishtowel and leave to rise in a warm place for about 1 hour until the dough has doubled in bulk.

4 Remove the dough from the bowl and place on a lightly floured surface. Knock back (punch down) the dough. Sprinkle a little more flour on the work surface and roll out the dough to a round about 30cm/12in in diameter.

5 Line a 23cm/9in flan tin (quiche pan) or dish with the dough. Gently press it into the tin or dish and trim off any overhanging pieces, leaving a 3mm/⅛in rim around the pastry case. Cover with a dishtowel, set aside in a warm place and leave to rise for about 30 minutes, or until puffy.

6 Meanwhile, melt the butter in a heavy pan and add the onion. Cover the pan and cook over a medium-low heat for about 15 minutes, until the onion has softened, stirring occasionally. Remove the lid and continue cooking, stirring frequently, until the onion is very soft and has caramelized.

7 Preheat the oven to 180°C/350°F/ Gas 4. Beat together the eggs and cream. Season and stir in the cooked onion.

8 Arrange the cheese on the base of the flan case. Pour over the egg mixture and bake for 30–35 minutes until the base is golden and the centre is just set. Cool slightly on a wire rack and serve warm with salad leaves.

EGG AND SPINACH PIE

THIS PIE WAS ORIGINALLY COOKED FOR GREEK EASTER CELEBRATIONS. IT IS TRADITIONALLY MADE WITH 33 LAYERS OF FILO PASTRY, EACH ONE REPRESENTING A YEAR OF CHRIST'S LIFE. IT MAKES AN EXCELLENT PICNIC DISH, AS IT CAN BE MADE IN ADVANCE AND TRAVELS WELL IN ITS COOKING TIN.

SERVES TEN TO TWELVE

INGREDIENTS
    oil, for greasing
    675g/1½lb fresh or frozen spinach,
      cooked and chopped
    115g/4oz/½ cup butter, melted
    1 bunch spring onions (scallions),
      finely chopped
    30ml/2 tbsp fresh marjoram, chopped
    350g/12oz/1½ cups ricotta cheese
    45ml/3 tbsp freshly grated
      Parmesan cheese
    60ml/4 tbsp double (heavy)
      cream, whipped
    5ml/1 tsp grated fresh nutmeg
    450g/1lb filo pastry
    2 egg whites, stiffly whisked
    8 eggs, hard-boiled (hard-cooked)
      and peeled
    salt and ground black pepper

1 Lightly grease a deep 20 × 25cm/ 8 × 10in roasting pan. Preheat the oven to 190ºC/375ºF/Gas 5.

2 Make sure the spinach is well cooked and thoroughly dried. Return it to the pan and cook gently, stirring until all the excess liquid has evaporated.

COOK'S TIP
This pie makes perfect picnic food. Partially cool it in the pan, then invert it on to a large board. Clean the pan and return the pie to the pan for easy transporting. You may find it easier to cut the pie into portions before going on your picnic.

3 Heat 30ml/2 tbsp butter in a pan and fry the spring onions until softened. Stir in the spinach and marjoram, and season with salt and ground black pepper to taste. Mix until well blended and the spinach is quite soft and smooth.

4 Place the ricotta, Parmesan, cream, nutmeg and seasoning in a bowl and beat until really smooth.

5 Use just over half the sheets of filo pastry for the base: brush each sheet with melted butter and layer neatly in the pan, allowing any excess pastry to hang over the edges. Filo pastry is very delicate, so you may find it simpler to cut very large sheets in half for easier handling. Keep the rest of the pastry covered with a damp cloth to prevent it from drying out.

VARIATION
For a pie with a slightly sharper, tangy taste, replace the ricotta cheese with the same weight of feta cheese. Crumble the cheese and mix with the cream, nutmeg and seasoning in step 4.

6 Whisk the egg whites, then fold into the cheese. Fold in the spinach until evenly mixed. Spoon half the mixture into the pan and arrange the eggs on top. Cover with the rest of the filling and fold over any excess pastry edges.

7 Brush the remaining sheets of pastry with butter and place over the top in an even layer. Brush with more butter, then bake for about 1 hour until the pastry is golden and the pie feels quite firm.

8 Allow the pie to cool slightly, then carefully invert it on to a clean surface and serve warm or leave to cool completely and serve cold.

ROASTED RATATOUILLE MOUSSAKA

BASED ON THE CLASSIC GREEK DISH, THIS MOUSSAKA REALLY HAS A TASTE OF THE MEDITERRANEAN. ROASTING BRINGS OUT THE DEEP RICH FLAVOURS OF THE VEGETABLES, WHICH GIVE A COLOURFUL CONTRAST TO THE LIGHT AND MOUTHWATERING EGG-AND-CHEESE TOPPING. THIS DISH IS PERFECT AS A HEARTY WINTER SIDE DISH OR AS A VEGETARIAN MAIN COURSE.

SERVES FOUR TO SIX

INGREDIENTS
  2 red (bell) peppers, seeded and cut
    into large chunks
  2 yellow (bell) peppers, seeded and
    cut into large chunks
  2 aubergines (eggplants), cut into
    large chunks
  3 courgettes (zucchini), thickly sliced
  45ml/3 tbsp olive oil
  3 garlic cloves, crushed
  400g/14oz can chopped tomatoes
  30ml/2 tbsp sun-dried tomato paste
  45ml/3 tbsp chopped fresh basil
  15ml/1 tbsp balsamic vinegar
  1.5ml/¼ tsp light brown sugar
  salt and ground black pepper
  basil leaves, to garnish
For the topping
  25g/1oz/2 tbsp butter
  25g/1oz/¼ cup plain (all-
    purpose) flour
  300ml/½ pint/1¼ cups milk
  1.5ml/¼ tsp freshly grated nutmeg
  250g/9oz/generous 1 cup
    ricotta cheese
  3 eggs, beaten
  25g/1oz/⅓ cup freshly grated
    Parmesan cheese

1 Preheat the oven to 230°C/450°F/ Gas 8. Arrange the peppers, aubergines and courgettes in an even layer in a large roasting pan. Season well with salt and ground black pepper.

2 Mix together the oil and crushed garlic cloves and pour them over the vegetables. Shake the roasting pan to coat the vegetables thoroughly in the garlic mixture.

3 Roast in the oven for 15–20 minutes until slightly charred, lightly tossing the vegetables once during the cooking time. Remove the pan from the oven and set aside. Reduce the oven temperature to 200°C/400°F/Gas 6.

4 Put the chopped tomatoes, sun-dried tomato paste, chopped basil, balsamic vinegar and brown sugar in a large, heavy pan and heat to boiling point. Reduce the heat and simmer gently, uncovered, for about 10–15 minutes until thickened, stirring occasionally. Season with salt and freshly ground black pepper to taste.

5 Carefully tip the roasted vegetables out of their pan and into the pan of tomato sauce. Mix well, coating the vegetables thoroughly in the tomato sauce. Spoon into an ovenproof dish.

6 To make the topping, melt the butter in a large, heavy pan over a gentle heat. Stir in the flour and cook for 1 minute. Pour in the milk, stirring constantly, then whisk until blended. Add the nutmeg and continue whisking over a gentle heat until thickened. Cook for a further 2 minutes, then remove from the heat and leave to cool slightly.

7 Mix in the ricotta cheese and beaten eggs thoroughly. Season with salt and plenty of freshly ground black pepper to taste.

8 Level the surface of the roasted vegetable mixture with the back of a spoon. Spoon the moussaka topping over the vegetables and sprinkle with the Parmesan cheese. Bake for 30–35 minutes until the topping is golden brown. Serve immediately, garnished with basil leaves.

VARIATION
Rather than baking this recipe in one large dish, divide the roasted vegetables and topping among individual gratin dishes. Reduce the baking time to 25 minutes. Individual portions can also be frozen and, when needed, simply removed from the freezer, left to thaw and baked for 30–35 minutes – ideal for those with a vegetarian in the family, or for unexpected guests.

BAKED HERB CRÊPES

TURN LIGHT HERB CRÊPES INTO SOMETHING SPECIAL. FILL WITH A SPINACH, CHEESE AND PINE NUT FILLING, THEN BAKE AND SERVE WITH A DELICIOUS TOMATO SAUCE.

SERVES FOUR

INGREDIENTS
    25g/1oz/⅔ cup chopped fresh herbs
    15ml/1 tbsp sunflower oil, plus extra
      for frying
    120ml/4fl oz/½ cup milk
    3 eggs
    25g/1oz/¼ cup plain (all-purpose) flour
    pinch of salt
For the sauce
    30ml/2 tbsp olive oil
    1 small onion, chopped
    2 garlic cloves, crushed
    400g/14oz can chopped tomatoes
    pinch of light brown sugar
For the filling
    450g/1lb fresh spinach, cooked
      and drained
    175g/6oz/¾ cup ricotta cheese
    25g/1oz/¼ cup pine nuts, toasted
    5 sun-dried tomato halves in olive
      oil, drained and chopped
    30ml/2 tbsp shredded fresh basil
    salt, nutmeg and ground black pepper
    4 egg whites
    oil, for greasing

1 To make the crêpes, place the herbs and oil in a food processor and blend until smooth. Add the milk, eggs, flour and salt and process again until smooth. Leave to rest for 30 minutes.

2 Heat a small non-stick frying pan and add a very small amount of oil. Pour out any excess oil and pour in a ladleful of the batter. Swirl to cover the base. Cook for 2 minutes, turn over and cook for a further 1 minute. Make the remaining seven crêpes in the same way.

3 To make the sauce, heat the oil in a small pan, add the onion and garlic and cook gently for 5 minutes. Add the tomatoes and sugar and cook for about 10 minutes until thickened. Process in a blender, then sieve and set aside.

4 To make the filling, mix together the spinach with the ricotta, pine nuts, tomatoes and basil. Season with salt, nutmeg and pepper.

5 Preheat the oven to 190°C/375°F/ Gas 5. Whisk the four egg whites until stiff. Fold one-third into the spinach mixture, then gently fold in the rest.

6 Place one crêpe at a time on a lightly oiled baking sheet, add a spoonful of filling and fold into quarters. Bake for 12 minutes until set. Reheat the sauce and serve with the crêpes.

BAKED COD WITH HOLLANDAISE SAUCE

SIMPLY COOKED FRESH FISH NEEDS LITTLE ASSISTANCE OTHER THAN A SPOONFUL OF CLASSIC HOLLANDAISE SAUCE. THIS RECIPE ALSO INCLUDES SOME VARIATIONS TO THE CLASSIC SAUCE.

SERVES FOUR

INGREDIENTS

   4 cod steaks or cutlets
   a little olive oil
   a squeeze of lemon juice
   15ml/1 tbsp fresh white breadcrumbs
   15ml/1 tbsp roughly ground hazelnuts
   salt and ground black pepper
   a few sprigs of dill, to garnish
   chips (French fries) and mixed leaf
     salad, to serve
For the sauce
   30ml/2 tbsp lemon juice
   2 egg yolks
   115g/4oz/½ cup butter, melted and
     cooled slightly

3 Whisk in the egg yolks, then, over a very gentle heat, add the butter in a slow stream, whisking all the time. Keep whisking until glossy and thick, then season to taste. Keep warm over a pan of hot water, until ready to serve.

4 Top the fish with the sauce and garnish with dill. Serve with chips and a mixed leaf salad.

VARIATIONS

To make anchovy sauce, whisk in 2–3 mashed anchovy fillets and keep whisking until they dissolve. Season after adding the anchovy. This sauce may only need pepper as anchovy fillets are very salty. To make herb sauce, whisk in 30ml/2 tbsp finely chopped fresh dill and leave to stand 5–10 minutes before serving for the flavour to come out. To make tomato hollandaise sauce, stir in 30ml/2 tbsp very finely chopped plum tomatoes and add extra pepper to taste.

1 Preheat the oven to 200°C/400°F/Gas 6. Brush both sides of the cod with oil and lemon juice. Season, then mix together the crumbs, nuts and seasoning and press on to the fish. Place on a baking sheet and bake for 20 minutes.

2 Meanwhile, prepare the hollandaise sauce. Simmer the lemon juice with 30ml/2 tbsp water in a small pan for a couple of minutes until reduced by at least half. Cool slightly.

GOAT'S CHEESE SOUFFLÉ

MAKE SURE EVERYONE IS SEATED BEFORE THIS SOUFFLÉ IS SERVED BECAUSE IT WILL BEGIN TO DEFLATE ALMOST IMMEDIATELY. THIS DISH IS DELICIOUS SERVED WITH A CRISP WHITE WINE.

2 Preheat the oven to 190°C/375°F/Gas 5. Butter a 1.5 litre/2½ pint/6¼ cup soufflé dish and sprinkle with Parmesan cheese. Remove the sauce from the heat and discard the bay leaf. Stir in the other cheeses.

3 In a clean grease-free bowl, using a balloon whisk or electric mixer, beat the egg whites slowly until they become frothy. Add the cream of tartar, increase the speed and continue beating until they form stiff peaks that just flop over a little at the top.

4 Stir a spoonful of beaten egg whites into the cheese sauce to lighten it, then pour the cheese sauce over the rest of the whites. Using a rubber spatula or large metal spoon, gently fold the sauce into the whites, cutting down through the centre to the bottom, then along the side of the bowl and up to the top, until the cheese sauce and egg whites are just combined.

SERVES FOUR

INGREDIENTS
25g/1oz/2 tbsp butter, plus extra
  for greasing
30ml/2 tbsp plain (all-purpose) flour
175ml/6fl oz/¾ cup milk
1 bay leaf
freshly grated nutmeg
freshly grated Parmesan cheese,
  for sprinkling
40g/1½oz herb and garlic soft cheese
150g/5oz/1¼ cups firm goat's
  cheese, diced
6 egg whites, at room temperature
1.5ml/¼ tsp cream of tartar
salt and ground black pepper

VARIATION
Use a blue cheese, such as Roquefort or Stilton, instead of goat's cheese.

1 Melt the butter in a heavy pan over a medium heat. Stir in the flour and cook until slightly golden, stirring constantly. Pour in half the milk, stir until smooth, then add the remaining milk and the bay leaf. Season with salt and plenty of pepper and nutmeg. Reduce the heat to medium-low, cover and simmer gently, stirring occasionally, for 5 minutes.

5 Gently pour the soufflé mixture into the prepared dish and bake for about 30 minutes until puffed and golden brown. Serve immediately.

SPINACH AND GOAT'S CHEESE ROULADE

THIS TWICE-BAKED ROULADE IS REALLY A ROLLED SOUFFLÉ. BECAUSE IT HAS AIR TRAPPED INSIDE, IT RISES AGAIN ON REHEATING AND BECOMES QUITE CRISP ON THE OUTSIDE.

SERVES FOUR

INGREDIENTS

300ml/½ pint/1¼ cups milk
50g/2oz/½ cup plain (all-purpose) flour
150g/5oz/⅔ cup butter
100g/3¾oz chèvre (goat's cheese), chopped
40g/1½oz/½ cup freshly grated Parmesan cheese, plus extra for dusting
4 eggs, separated
250g/9oz/2¼ cups fresh shiitake mushrooms, sliced
275g/10oz baby spinach leaves, washed
45ml/3 tbsp crème fraîche
salt and ground black pepper

1 Preheat the oven to 190°C/375°F/ Gas 5. Line a 30 × 20cm/12 × 8in Swiss-roll tin (jelly roll pan) with greaseproof (waxed) paper, making sure that the edge of the paper rises well above the sides of the tin. Grease lightly.

2 Combine the milk, flour and 50g/2oz/ ¼ cup of the butter in a pan. Bring to the boil over a low heat, whisking until thick. Lower the heat and simmer for 2 minutes, then mix in the chèvre and half the Parmesan. Cool for 5 minutes, then beat in the egg yolks. Season.

3 Whisk the egg whites in a grease-free bowl until soft peaks form. Carefully fold the whites into the chèvre mixture, using a large metal spoon. Spoon the mixture into the prepared tin, spread gently to level, then bake for about 15 minutes until the top feels just firm.

4 Let the roulade cool for a short time. Meanwhile, dust a sheet of greaseproof paper with a little Parmesan cheese and carefully invert the roulade on to the paper. Tear the lining paper away from the base of the roulade, in strips. Roll up in the greaseproof paper and set aside to cool completely.

5 To make the filling, melt the rest of the butter in a pan, reserving 30ml/2 tbsp. Add the mushrooms and stir-fry for 3 minutes. In a separate pan, cook the spinach until it wilts. Drain well, add to the mushrooms and stir in the crème fraîche. Season, then cool. Preheat the oven to the original temperature.

6 Unroll the roulade and spread over the filling. Roll it up again and place on a baking sheet. Brush with the reserved butter and sprinkle with the remaining Parmesan. Bake for 15 minutes until risen and golden. Serve immediately.

PARTY FOODS AND DRINKS

Beautifully presented and delicious-tasting food and drink are all that a party needs to make it a success. This chapter provides a whole host of hot and cold snacks and nibbles. Dishes such as Tapenade and Quail's Egg Canapés and Eggs Mimosa, can be made well in advance and will make a beautiful centrepiece on any table. Hot party food, such as Prawn and Tomato Canapés and Cheese Aigrettes, can also be prepared ahead of time and need only a little last-minute cooking. They are sure to impress your guests and get them in the party mood. Also included are a tempting selection of unusual egg-based party drinks, such as Brandied Eggnog and Old-fashioned Lemonade, as well as the classic morning-after remedy, Prairie Oyster.

TAPENADE AND QUAIL'S EGG CANAPÉS

POPULARLY USED IN MEDITERRANEAN COOKING, TAPENADE IS A PURÉE MADE FROM CAPERS, OLIVES AND ANCHOVIES. ITS STRONG FLAVOUR PERFECTLY COMPLEMENTS THE TASTE OF EGGS, ESPECIALLY QUAIL'S EGGS, WHICH LOOK VERY PRETTY ON THE OPEN SANDWICHES.

3 Arrange a little frisée lettuce and a slice of tomato on top of each piece of bread.

4 Halve the quail's eggs and place half on top of each tomato slice.

5 Top each egg with a quartered olive and a halved anchovy fillet and garnish with chopped parsley.

SERVES EIGHT

INGREDIENTS
  4 quail's eggs
  1 small baguette
  45ml/3 tbsp tapenade
  a few leaves of frisée lettuce
  3 small tomatoes, sliced and halved
  4 canned anchovy fillets,
    halved lengthways
  2 black olives, pitted and quartered
  chopped fresh parsley, to garnish

COOK'S TIP
For a crunchier base, brush each slice of bread with olive oil and grill (broil) on both sides until crisp and golden.

1 Place the quail's eggs in a pan of cold water, bring to the boil and cook for 3 minutes. Leave to cool, then peel.

2 Cut the baguette into eight slices, on the diagonal, and spread with tapenade.

VARIATION
Make a tuna tapenade filling for hard-boiled (hard-cooked) eggs. Put a 90g/ 3½oz can drained tuna in a food processor with 25g/1oz capers, 75g/3oz pitted black olives and 10 canned anchovy fillets and blend until smooth, scraping down the sides as necessary. Gradually add 60ml/4 tbsp olive oil through the feeder tube and combine. To fill the eggs, blend the tuna tapenade with the egg yolks then, using a teaspoon, pile the mixture into the halved egg whites.

CHEESE AIGRETTES

CHOUX PASTRY IS OFTEN USED TO MAKE SWEET PASTRIES, SUCH AS PROFITEROLES, BUT THESE LITTLE SAVOURY BUNS, FLAVOURED WITH GRUYÈRE AND DUSTED WITH GRATED PARMESAN, ARE JUST DELICIOUS. THEY MAKE A WONDERFUL PARTY SNACK AND ARE BEST MADE AHEAD OF TIME AND DEEP FRIED TO SERVE.

MAKES THIRTY

INGREDIENTS
    100g/3¾oz/scant 1 cup plain (all-
      purpose) flour
    2.5ml/½ tsp paprika
    2.5ml/½ tsp salt
    75g/3oz/6 tbsp cold butter, diced
    3 eggs, beaten
    75g/3oz/¾ cup coarsely grated
      mature (sharp) Gruyère cheese
    corn oil, for deep-frying
    50g/2oz/⅔ cup freshly grated
      Parmesan cheese
    ground black pepper

1 Mix together the flour, paprika and salt by sifting them on to a sheet of greaseproof (waxed) paper. Add a generous grinding of black pepper.

2 Put the butter and 200ml/7fl oz/scant 1 cup water into a pan and heat gently. As soon as the butter has melted and the liquid starts to boil, tip in all the seasoned flour at once and beat hard with a wooden spoon until the mixture forms a stiff paste and comes away from the sides of the pan in a ball.

3 Remove the pan from the heat and cool the paste for 5 minutes. This is important if the aigrettes are to rise well. Gradually beat in enough of the beaten egg to give a stiff dropping (pourable) consistency that still holds a shape on the spoon. Mix in the Gruyère.

4 Heat the oil for deep-frying to 180°C/ 350°F or until hot enough to turn a cube of bread brown in 1 minute. Take a teaspoonful of the choux paste and use a second spoon to slide it into the oil. Make more aigrettes in the same way. Fry for 3–4 minutes until golden brown. Drain on kitchen paper and keep warm while cooking successive batches. To serve, pile the aigrettes on a warmed serving dish and sprinkle with Parmesan.

VARIATION
Filling these aigrettes gives your guests a delightful surprise as they bite through the crisp shell. Make slightly larger aigrettes by dropping larger spoonfuls of dough into the hot oil and cooking for 1–2 minutes more. Slit them open and scoop out any soft paste that remains inside. Fill the centres with taramasalata or crumbled Roquefort mixed with a little fromage frais or natural (plain) yogurt.

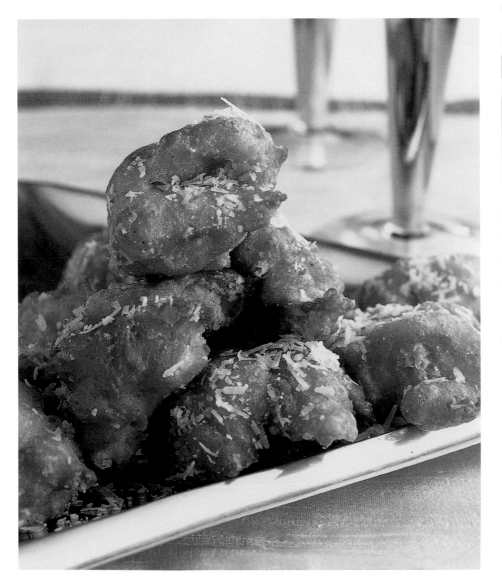

EGG CANAPÉS

THESE ELEGANT PARTY PIECES TAKE A LITTLE TIME TO MAKE, BUT THEY CAN BE PREPARED IN ADVANCE WITH THE FINAL TOUCHES ADDED JUST BEFORE YOUR GUESTS ARRIVE.

EACH VARIATION MAKES 12

TRUFFLE CANAPÉS
INGREDIENTS
    225g/8oz shortcrust
      (unsweetened) pastry
    2 eggs, beaten
    15g/½oz/1 tbsp butter
    5ml/1 tsp truffle oil
    salt and ground black pepper
    chopped chives, to garnish

1 Preheat the oven to 190°C/375°F/ Gas 5. Roll out the pastry very thinly on a floured surface and line 12 very small tartlet or muffin tins (pans).

2 Line the base of each pastry case (shell) with greaseproof (waxed) paper and bake for 10 minutes. Remove the paper and bake for a further 5 minutes until the pastry is crisp and golden.

3 Season the beaten eggs, then melt the butter in a pan, pour in the eggs and stir constantly over a gentle heat. When the eggs are almost set, stir in the truffle oil. Spoon the mixture into the pastry cases and top with chives. Serve warm or cold.

PRAWN AND TOMATO CANAPÉS
INGREDIENTS
    225g/8oz shortcrust
      (unsweetened) pastry
    2 tomatoes, peeled and chopped
    12 large cooked prawns (shrimp),
      peeled but tails left on
    60ml/4 tbsp hollandaise sauce
    salt and ground black pepper
    fennel or chervil sprigs, to garnish

1 Preheat the oven to 190°C/375°F/ Gas 5. Roll out the pastry very thinly on a floured surface and line 12 very small tartlet or muffin tins (pans).

2 Line the base of each pastry case (shell) with greaseproof (waxed) paper and bake for 10 minutes. Remove the paper and bake for 5 minutes more.

3 Place some chopped tomato in the base of each tartlet and season with salt and pepper. Top with the prawns and spoon on some hollandaise sauce. Warm through briefly in the oven and serve garnished with fennel or chervil.

WATERCRESS AND AVOCADO CANAPÉS
INGREDIENTS
    3–4 slices dark rye bread
    1 small ripe avocado
    15ml/1 tbsp lemon juice
    45ml/3 tbsp mayonnaise
    ½ bunch watercress, chopped,
      reserving a few sprigs to garnish
    6 quail's eggs, hard-boiled
      (hard-cooked)

1 Cut the bread into 12 rounds, using a plain or fluted biscuit (cookie) cutter.

2 Cut the avocado in half, around the stone (pit). Peel half, then slice and dip each piece in lemon juice. Put a piece of avocado on each bread round.

3 Scoop the remaining avocado into a bowl and mash. Mix in the mayonnaise and watercress. Spoon a little of the mixture on to each canapé, top with a peeled, halved quail's egg and garnish with a sprig of watercress.

SALMON AND CORIANDER CANAPÉS
INGREDIENTS
    3–4 slices dark rye bread
    2 eggs, hard-boiled (hard-cooked)
      and thinly sliced
    115g/4oz poached salmon
    coriander (cilantro) leaves, to garnish
For the lime mayonnaise
    45–60ml/3–4 tbsp mayonnaise
    5ml/1 tsp chopped fresh
      coriander (cilantro)
    5ml/1 tsp lime juice
    salt and ground black pepper

1 Cut the rye bread into 12 triangular pieces, using a sharp knife.

2 Make the lime mayonnaise. Combine the mayonnaise, coriander and lime juice in a small bowl. Season with salt and pepper to taste.

3 Top each bread triangle with a slice of egg, a small portion of salmon and a teaspoon of mayonnaise. Garnish with a coriander leaf. Chill until ready to serve.

MARBLED EGGS

THESE EGGS ARE COLOURED WITH TEA LEAVES, AN ASIAN METHOD THAT GIVES A VERY SUBTLE TASTE.
YOU COULD ALSO USE THE SKINS OF 3–4 ONIONS, WHICH TENDS TO GIVE A STRONGER, MORE
SAVOURY FLAVOUR TO THE EGGS.

SERVES FOUR

INGREDIENTS
   4 eggs
   30ml/2 tbsp dry strong tea leaves
   5ml/1 tsp salt
   2 star anise
   2–3 cardamom pods
For the Thai fish sauce
   2 red chillies, finely chopped
   2 garlic cloves, crushed
   45ml/3 tbsp hoisin sauce
   15ml/1 tbsp soy sauce
   15ml/1 tbsp fish sauce

COOK'S TIP
For extra flavour, add a little soy sauce to
the tea before adding the eggs.

1 Place the eggs in a pan of cold water,
bring to the boil and cook for about
5 minutes. Cool, then crack the shells
all over. Return to the pan with the tea
and seasonings, add water to cover and
bring to the boil. Simmer for 1½ hours,
then cool in the water and peel.

2 To make the Thai fish sauce, pound the
chillies and garlic to a paste in a mortar,
then blend in the rest of the sauce
ingredients, discarding the chilli seeds,
if you prefer a milder flavour. Chill until
required. Serve the sauce with the eggs,
or use as a garnish.

PICKLED QUAIL'S EGGS

THESE CHINESE EGGS ARE PICKLED IN ALCOHOL AND CAN BE STORED IN A PRESERVING JAR IN A COOL DARK PLACE FOR SEVERAL MONTHS. THEY MAKE DELICIOUS BITESIZE SNACKS AT DRINKS PARTIES AND ARE SURE TO DELIGHT GUESTS.

SERVES TWELVE

INGREDIENTS
    12 quail's eggs
    15ml/1 tbsp salt
    750ml/1¼ pints/3 cups distilled
      or boiled water
    5ml/1 tsp Sichuan peppercorns
    150ml/¼ pint/⅔ cup spirit,
      such as Mou-tai (Chinese brandy),
      brandy, whisky, rum or vodka
    dipping sauce (see Cook's Tips) and
      toasted sesame seeds, to
      serve (optional)

1 Place the eggs in a pan of gently simmering water, bring to the boil and cook for 3 minutes until the yolks are soft, but not runny. Remove the eggs from the pan using a slotted spoon and set aside to cool.

2 In a large pan, dissolve the salt in the distilled or boiled water. Add the peppercorns, then allow the water to cool and add the spirit.

COOK'S TIPS
• Although you can buy Chinese dipping sauces in the supermarket, it is very easy to make your own at home. To make a quick dipping sauce, mix together equal quantities of soy sauce and hoisin sauce in a small bowl.
• Be sure to use only boiled or distilled water for the eggs. The water must be completely free of harmful bacteria because they can enter through the eggs' porous shells.

3 Gently tap the eggs all over to crack the shells but do not peel them. Place in a large, airtight, sterilized jar and fill up with the liquid, totally covering the eggs. Seal the jar and leave to stand in a cool, dark place for at least 7 days.

4 To serve, remove the eggs from the liquid and carefully peel off the shells. Serve whole with a dipping sauce and a bowl of toasted sesame seeds or cut each egg in half or quarters and serve as a garnish.

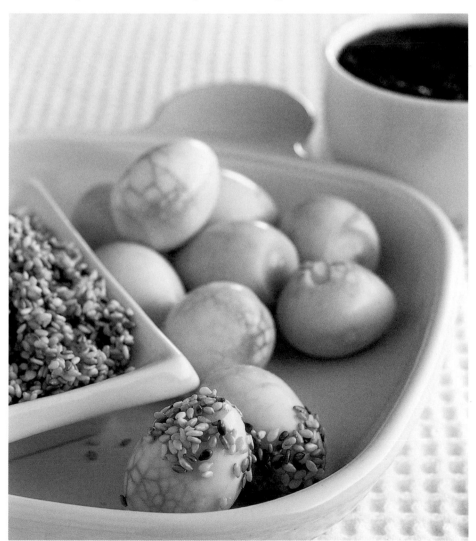

ROLLED OMELETTE

JAPANESE FOOD IS ALWAYS PREPARED AND SERVED WITH PRECISION AND ELEGANCE. THIS FIRMLY SET, ROLLED OMELETTE IS CUT INTO NEAT PIECES, SHOWING THE EXQUISITE LAYERING INSIDE. THE TEXTURE SHOULD BE SMOOTH AND SOFT, NOT LEATHERY, AND THE FLAVOUR IS SWEET-SAVOURY. SOY SAUCE IS THE PERFECT CONDIMENT TO COMPLEMENT ITS FLAVOUR AND TEXTURE.

SERVES FOUR

INGREDIENTS
  8 eggs
  60ml/4 tbsp sugar
  20ml/4 tsp soy sauce
  90ml/6 tbsp sake or dry
   white wine
  vegetable oil, for cooking
  soy sauce or plum sauce, to serve
For the garnish
  8cm/3¼in piece of mooli
   (daikon), finely grated
  shiso leaves (optional)

1 Break the eggs into a large bowl, mix them together, using a pair of chopsticks and a cutting action.

2 In a small bowl, mix together the sugar with the soy sauce and sake or dry white wine. Lightly stir this mixture into the beaten eggs. Divide the mixture between two bowls so that it can be cooked in equal batches.

3 Heat a little oil in a medium-size frying pan and carefully wipe out the excess with kitchen paper.

COOK'S TIPS
Japanese ginger pickles can be found in chiller compartments in good supermarkets or in specialist food stores. They have a refreshing, zesty flavour, which complements this omelette perfectly.

4 Pour a quarter of the mixture from one bowl into the frying pan, tilting it to coat the base in a thin layer. When the edge has set, but the middle is still moist, roll up the egg towards you.

5 Moisten a piece of kitchen paper with oil and grease the empty side of the pan. Pour in a third of the remaining egg mixture and lift up the rolled egg with your chopsticks to let the raw egg run underneath.

6 When the edges have set, roll up the omelette in the opposite direction, tilting the pan away from you so that the omelette rolls easily.

7 Slide the roll towards you again, grease the pan, using the oily kitchen paper. Pour half of the remaining egg mixture into the pan, lifting the egg roll and allowing the uncooked egg to run under it as before.

8 When set, insert the chopsticks in the side of the rolled omelette and flip it over towards the opposite side of the frying pan. Add the remaining egg and cook in the same way. Slide the roll so that the join is underneath. Cook for a further 10 seconds.

9 Slide the roll out on to a bamboo mat, if you have one, and roll up tightly, then press neatly into a rectangular shape. If you don't have a bamboo mat, simply press the omelette into a rectangle using your hands. Leave to cool.

10 Cook the remaining batch of egg mixture in the same way to make a second omelette roll. Slice the cold omelettes into 2.5cm/1in thick pieces, garnish with mooli and shiso leaves. Serve with soy or plum sauce.

EGGS MIMOSA

THE USE OF THE WORD MIMOSA DESCRIBES THE FINE YELLOW AND WHITE GRATED EGG, WHICH LOOKS VERY SIMILAR TO THE FLOWER OF THE SAME NAME. THIS PRETTY GARNISH CAN BE USED TO FINISH ANY DISH AND ADDS A LIGHT, SUMMERY TOUCH.

MAKES TWENTY-FOUR

INGREDIENTS
    12 eggs, hard-boiled (hard-cooked)
      and peeled
    2 ripe avocados, halved and
      stoned (pitted)
    1 garlic clove, crushed
    a few drops of Tabasco sauce
    15ml/1 tbsp extra virgin olive oil
    salt and ground black pepper
    basil leaves, to garnish

COOK'S TIP
You can prepare the mimosa garnish in advance, but store the egg white and yolk separately, in small airtight containers, and keep them chilled.

1 Reserve two of the hard-boiled eggs and halve the remaining ones. Carefully remove the yolks with a teaspoon and blend together with the avocados, garlic, Tabasco sauce, oil and seasoning. Pipe or spoon the mixture into the halved egg whites.

2 Sieve the remaining egg whites and sprinkle over the filled eggs. Sieve the yolks on top. Arrange the filled egg halves on a serving platter. Sprinkle a little ground black pepper over the eggs and sprinkle with basil leaves to garnish, then serve.

CHEESE-CRUSTED PARTY EGGS

SIMILAR TO THE POPULAR SCOTCH EGG, THESE WHOLE SMALL EGGS ARE WRAPPED IN A DELICIOUS VEGETARIAN COATING, THEN DEEP-FRIED. THEY KEEP WELL FOR SEVERAL DAYS AND MAKE VERY GOOD PARTY SNACKS. THEY ARE ALSO IDEAL AS PICNIC AND TRAVEL FOOD.

MAKES SIX

INGREDIENTS
115g/4oz/1⅔ cups stale
  white breadcrumbs
½ small leek, very finely chopped
115g/4oz/1 cup grated mild but
  tasty cheese
5ml/1 tsp garlic and herb seasoning
30ml/2 tbsp chopped fresh parsley
5ml/1 tsp mild mustard
2 eggs, separated
30–45ml/2–3 tbsp milk
6 small spinach or sorrel leaves,
  stalks removed
6 small eggs, such as bantam, guinea
  fowl, or 8–10 quail's eggs, hard-
  boiled (hard-cooked) and peeled
25–40g/1–1½oz/¼–⅓ cup flour,
  for coating, plus extra for dusting
25g/1oz/2 tbsp sesame seeds,
  for coating
oil, for deep-frying
salt and ground black pepper
mayonnaise, to serve

1 Mix together the breadcrumbs, leeks, cheese, seasoning, parsley and mustard. Beat together the egg yolks and milk and blend into the mixture. Whisk one egg white until quite stiff and gradually work sufficient stiff egg white into the breadcrumb mixture to give a firm, dropping (pouring) consistency. Chill for about 1 hour.

COOK'S TIP
Make sure that you coat the eggs evenly first with the egg whites and then with the sesame flour to seal them completely.

2 Divide the mixture into six. Mould one portion in the palm of your hand, place a spinach leaf inside and then an egg and carefully shape the mixture around the egg to enclose it within a thin crust. Seal well and dust lightly with flour. Repeat with the remainder.

3 Beat the remaining egg white with 15ml/1 tbsp water, then pour into a shallow dish. Mix the flour with salt and pepper and the sesame seeds and place in another shallow dish. Dip the eggs first in the beaten egg white, then in the sesame flour. Cover and chill for at least 20 minutes.

4 Heat the oil in a pan until a crust of bread turns golden in about 1¼ minutes. Deep-fry the eggs in the hot oil, turning frequently, until golden brown all over. Remove with a slotted spoon, drain on kitchen paper and leave to cool. Serve, sliced in half, with a bowl of good-quality mayonnaise for dipping.

PARMESAN THINS

These melt-in-the-mouth morsels are very more-ish, so make plenty. Don't just keep them for parties — they make a great snack at any time of the day.

MAKES SIXTEEN TO TWENTY

INGREDIENTS
    50g/2oz/½ cup plain (all-purpose) flour
    40g/1½oz/3 tbsp butter, softened
    1 egg yolk
    40g/1½oz/⅔ cup freshly grated
        Parmesan cheese
    pinch each of salt and
        mustard powder

COOK'S TIP
If you want to make large quantities of these biscuits (crackers), freeze the dough in logs, wrapped in foil. To thaw, remove from the freezer and leave for at least 1 hour before cutting and baking.

1 Rub together the flour and the butter in a bowl, then work in the egg yolk, cheese, salt and mustard. Mix to bring the dough together into a ball. Shape into a log, then wrap in foil or clear film (plastic wrap) and chill in the refrigerator for at least 10 minutes.

2 Preheat the oven to 200°C/400°F/Gas 6. Cut the dough log into very thin slices, about 3–6mm/⅛–¼in, and arrange on a baking tray. Flatten with a fork to give a pretty ridged pattern. Bake for 10 minutes or until crisp. Cool on a wire rack.

ELEGANT EGG SANDWICHES

A WELL-MADE EGG SANDWICH IS ONE OF THE BEST AND QUICKEST SNACKS. HERE ARE TWO FAVOURITE FILLINGS, DELICIOUS AT ANY TIME OF DAY.

SERVES SIX

INGREDIENTS
    12 thin slices white or brown
      bread, crusts removed
    50g/2oz/4 tbsp butter, at
      room temperature
    slices of lemon,
      to garnish
For the egg and cress filling
    2 small hard-boiled (hard-cooked)
      eggs, peeled and finely chopped
    30ml/2 tbsp mayonnaise
    ½ small box cress
    salt and ground black pepper
For the egg and tuna filling
    2 small hard-boiled (hard-cooked)
      eggs, peeled and finely chopped
    25g/1oz canned tuna in oil, drained
      and mashed
    5ml/1 tsp paprika
    squeeze of lemon juice
    25g/1oz piece cucumber, peeled
      and thinly sliced

1 Carefully trim the crusts off the bread, using a sharp knife, then spread the bread thinly with softened butter.

VARIATION
For harlequin sandwiches, use a combination of white and brown bread. Use a slice of brown bread for one side of each sandwich and a slice of white for the other. Arrange them on a plate, turning the sandwiches to show alternate brown and white sides.

2 To make the egg and cress filling, mix the chopped eggs with the mayonnaise, cress and seasoning. Layer between six slices of bread. Press down gently and cut into neat triangles.

COOK'S TIP
These sandwiches will keep well for 2–3 hours. Cover with damp kitchen paper, then cover tightly in clear film (plastic wrap). Chill until required.

3 To make the egg and tuna filling, mix the chopped eggs with the tuna, paprika, lemon juice and seasoning. Put cucumber on three slices of bread, top with the tuna mixture and the rest of the bread. Press down lightly and cut each sandwich into three neat fingers.

4 Arrange all the sandwiches on a plate and garnish with lemon slices.

BANANA AND MAPLE FLIP

THIS NOURISHING AND HEALTHY BREAKFAST DRINK IS PACKED WITH SO MUCH GOODNESS THAT YOU WON'T NEED ANYTHING ELSE FOR YOUR MORNING MEAL, BUT IT IS PERFECT FOR A BRUNCH PARTY. AS IT IS MADE WITH A RAW EGG, DO BE SURE TO USE A REALLY FRESH FREE-RANGE ONE.

SERVES ONE

INGREDIENTS
   1 small banana, peeled and halved
   50g/2oz/¼ cup thick Greek
     (US strained plain) yogurt
   1 egg
   30ml/2 tbsp maple syrup
   5ml/1 tsp lemon juice
   2 ice cubes
   slice of orange, to serve (optional)

COOK'S TIPS
• To chill the glass quickly, place it in the freezer while you are preparing the drink.
• If your food processor isn't a heavy-duty model, crush the ice cubes first.

1 Put the banana, yogurt, egg, maple syrup, lemon juice and the ice cubes into a food processor or blender.

2 Blend continuously for 2 minutes until the mixture becomes really pale and frothy.

3 Pour into a tall, chilled glass and top with a slice of orange, if you like.

VARIATION
For a different fruity flavour, substitute a small, very ripe, peeled, stoned (pitted) and chopped mango for the banana.

PRAIRIE OYSTER

BASED ON THE ORIGINAL MORNING-AFTER DRINK, WHICH IS TRADITIONALLY SERVED WITH A LARGE MEASURE OF SPIRITS, THIS IS A NON-ALCOHOLIC VERSION, ALTHOUGH YOU CAN ALWAYS ADD A SMALL SPLASH OF BRANDY IF YOU REALLY FEEL THE NEED. THE DRINK CONTAINS A RAW EGG YOLK SO DO BE SURE TO USE A FRESH ONE (SEE WATCHPOINT, BELOW).

SERVES ONE

INGREDIENTS
   5ml/1 tsp Worcestershire
     sauce
   5ml/1 tsp white wine vinegar
   5ml/1 tsp tomato ketchup
     or tomato sauce
   1 egg yolk, unbroken
   cayenne pepper

WATCHPOINT
The very young, the elderly, pregnant women and those in ill-health or with a compromised immune system are advised against consuming raw eggs or dishes and drinks containing raw eggs. This is because salmonella bacteria, which can cause severe food poisoning, are sometimes found in eggs and poultry. The bacteria are destroyed when eggs are heated to a temperature of 60°C/125°F.

1 Place the Worcestershire sauce, white wine vinegar and tomato ketchup or tomato sauce in a tall, narrow glass and mix together, using a long-handled spoon or stirrer.

2 Carefully slide the unbroken egg yolk into the glass, but do not stir. Sprinkle in a little cayenne pepper and down the whole lot in a single gulp.

COOK'S TIP
If you don't like the idea of swallowing a whole raw egg yolk, try processing all the ingredients in a food processor or blender with some freshly squeezed orange juice.

OLD-FASHIONED LEMONADE

SERVES TWO

INGREDIENTS
a few large strips of lemon rind
75ml/5 tbsp lemon juice
50–75g/2–3oz/¼–generous ⅓ cup
    sugar, or to taste
2 egg whites
300ml/½ pint/1¼ cups boiling water
75ml/5 tbsp sherry
ice cubes, to serve
mint or lemon balm, to decorate

COOK'S TIP
Experiment with different flavours by replacing the sherry with another fortified wine, such as Madeira or vermouth.

1 Put the lemon rind and juice, sugar and egg whites into a bowl or large jug (pitcher). Whisk until frothy.

2 Whisk in the water and whisk for a further 2 minutes, until the sugar has dissolved completely.

3 Pour in the sherry, a little at a time, and whisk after each addition.

4 To serve, put several ice cubes into each of two tall glasses, pour over the lemonade and decorate the glasses with a sprig of mint or lemon balm.

BRANDIED EGGNOG

FOR INSOMNIACS, THIS FROTHY BLEND OF EGGS, MILK AND BRANDY WORKS WONDERS.

SERVES FOUR

INGREDIENTS

4 eggs, separated
25g/1oz/2 tbsp caster
   (superfine) sugar
120ml/4fl oz/½ cup brandy
300ml/½ pint/1¼ cups milk (or
   according to the volume of the
   glasses), heated to just below
   boiling point
freshly grated nutmeg

COOK'S TIP
To make a cold version, use chilled
single (light) cream instead of hot milk.
Sprinkle with finely grated chocolate.

1 Beat the egg yolks in a bowl with the
sugar. Beat the egg whites to soft peaks
in a separate bowl.

2 Fold together the yolks and whites
and pour into four heatproof glasses.

3 Pour 30ml/2 tbsp of brandy into each
heatproof glass.

4 Top up the glasses with hot milk.
Grate a little nutmeg over the top of
each and serve immediately.

COLD DESSERTS

Many classic cold desserts depend on eggs for their light, rich or creamy textures. Whisked egg whites create the crisp, yet chewy, texture of pavlova, while the same whisked egg whites also create the light and creamy delight of Frozen Grand Marnier Soufflés. Combining egg whites with egg yolks can also produce the divinely fruity Iced Mousse with Hot Pineapple, as well as Chocolate Chestnut Roulade. A classic egg custard is often used as the base of cold desserts. Banana with Apricot Caramel Trifle is layered with thick fresh custard, while in Rich Vanilla Ice Cream the creamy vanilla custard is frozen to make a perennially popular dessert. Classic baked custards include Baked Custard with Burnt Sugar and Passion Fruit Creams.

BAKED CUSTARD WITH BURNT SUGAR

THIS DESSERT IS THOUGHT TO HAVE ORIGINATED IN ENGLAND IN THE 18TH CENTURY AND HAS STOOD THE TEST OF TIME WELL. THE SOFT AND CREAMY EGG CUSTARD IS FLAVOURED WITH VANILLA AND TOPPED WITH A BRITTLE CARAMELIZED SUGAR CRUST.

SERVES SIX

INGREDIENTS

    1 vanilla pod (bean)
    1 litre/1¾ pints/4 cups double
      (heavy) cream
    6 egg yolks
    90g/3½oz/½ cup caster
      (superfine) sugar
    30ml/2 tbsp almond liqueur
    75g/3oz/⅓ cup soft light brown sugar

1 Preheat the oven to 150°C/300°F/ Gas 2. Place six 125ml/4fl oz/½ cup ramekins in a roasting pan or ovenproof dish and set aside.

2 Split the vanilla pod and scrape the seeds into a pan. Add the cream and bring just to the boil, stirring frequently. Remove from the heat and cover. Set aside for 15–20 minutes.

3 In a bowl, whisk the egg yolks, caster sugar and almond liqueur until well blended. Whisk in the hot cream and strain into a large jug (pitcher). Divide the custard among the ramekins.

4 Pour enough boiling water into the roasting pan to come halfway up the sides of the ramekins. Cover the pan with foil and bake for about 30 minutes until the custards are just set. To test whether the custards are ready, push the point of a knife into the centre of one – if it comes out clean, the custards are cooked. Remove the ramekins from the pan and leave to cool. Return to the dry roasting pan and chill.

5 Preheat the grill (broiler). Sprinkle the sugar over the surface of each custard and grill (broil) for 30–60 seconds until the sugar melts and caramelizes, taking care not to let the sugar burn. Place in the refrigerator to set the crust.

COOK'S TIP
It is best to make the custards the day before you wish to eat them, so that they can become really cold and firm.

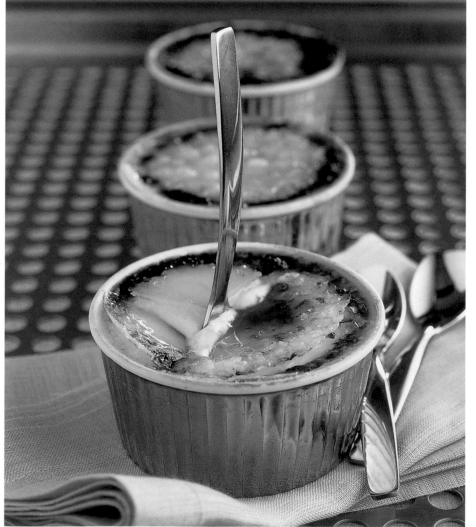

PASSION FRUIT CREAMS

THESE DELICATELY PERFUMED CREAMS ARE VERY LIGHT AND THE PASSION FRUIT GIVES THEM A REFRESHING, CITRUSY FLAVOUR.

SERVES FIVE TO SIX

INGREDIENTS
  butter, for greasing
  600ml/1 pint/2½ cups double (heavy)
    cream, or a mixture of single (light)
    and double (heavy) cream
  a few drops of vanilla essence (extract)
  6 passion fruits
  30–45ml/2–3 tbsp caster
    (superfine) sugar
  5 eggs
  30ml/2 tbsp lemon curd
  clotted cream and mint or
    geranium leaves, to serve

VARIATIONS
You can also serve these creams hot,
straight from their dishes, with an extra
passion fruit half on the side. To make a
crème caramel-style dessert, coat each
ramekin with caramel instead of paper.

1 Preheat the oven to 180°C/350°F/
Gas 4. Butter six ramekins and place a
circle of greaseproof (waxed) paper in
the bases. Place them in a roasting pan.

2 Bring the cream and vanilla to boiling
point. Sieve the flesh of four passion
fruits and beat together with the sugar,
eggs and lemon curd. Whisk in the hot
cream. Ladle into the ramekins and half
fill the roasting pan with boiling water.

3 Bake the creams for 25–30 minutes
or until they are just set. Remove from
the roasting pan and set aside to cool
before chilling in the refrigerator.

4 Run a knife around the insides of the
creams, then invert them on to serving
plates, tapping the bases firmly. Peel off
the greaseproof paper and chill. Just
before serving, spoon on a little passion
fruit flesh and add a herb leaf.

FLOATING ISLANDS

THE FRENCH NAME FOR THIS DISH IS OEUFS À LA NEIGE, MEANING SNOW EGGS. TRADITIONALLY THE MERINGUES ARE POACHED IN MILK, WHICH IS THEN USED TO MAKE THE RICH CUSTARD SAUCE. HOWEVER, THIS METHOD USES WATER FOR POACHING, WHICH GIVES A LIGHTER RESULT.

SERVES FOUR TO SIX

INGREDIENTS
  1 vanilla pod (bean)
  600ml/1 pint/2½ cups milk
  8 egg yolks
  200g/7oz/1 cup granulated sugar
For the meringues
  4 large (US extra large) egg whites
  1.5ml/¼ tsp cream
    of tartar
  225g/8oz/1¼ cups caster
    (superfine) sugar

1 Using a knife with a sharp point, carefully split the vanilla pod lengthways and scrape the tiny black seeds into a pan. Add the milk and bring to the boil over a medium-high heat, stirring frequently. Remove the pan from the heat and cover with a lid. Set aside for 15–20 minutes to cool slightly.

2 In a medium bowl, whisk the egg yolks and 50g/2oz/¼ cup of the sugar for 2–3 minutes until thick and creamy. Remove the vanilla pod from the hot milk, then whisk the milk into the egg mixture and return to the pan.

3 With a wooden spoon, stir the sauce over a medium-low heat until it begins to thicken and coats the back of the spoon; do not allow the custard to boil or it may curdle.

4 Strain the custard into a chilled bowl, leave to cool, stirring occasionally, then chill until ready to serve.

5 Half-fill a large frying pan or wide pan with water and bring just to simmering point. In a clean grease-free bowl, whisk the egg whites slowly until they are frothy. Add the cream of tartar, increase the speed and continue whisking until they form soft peaks. Gradually sprinkle over the caster sugar, about 30ml/2 tbsp at a time, and whisk until the whites are stiff and glossy.

6 Using two tablespoons, form egg-shaped meringues and slide them into the water – you may need to work in batches. Poach them for 2–3 minutes, turning once, until the meringue is just firm. Use a slotted spoon to transfer the meringues from the pan to a baking sheet lined with kitchen paper to drain.

7 Pour the cold custard into shallow individual serving dishes or plates and arrange the meringues on top.

8 To make the caramel to decorate, put the remaining sugar into a small heavy pan with 45ml/3 tbsp of water. Bring the dampened sugar to the boil over a high heat, carefully swirling the pan to dissolve it. Do not allow to boil until the sugar is completely dissolved, then boil, without stirring, until the syrup turns a dark caramel colour.

9 Working quickly before it hardens, drizzle the caramel over the poached meringues and custard in a zig-zag pattern. Serve cold.

COOK'S TIP
Do not make the caramel too far ahead or it will soften as it sits on the moist meringues. If you do not have a vanilla pod, you can use 5ml/1 tsp vanilla essence (extract) instead.

BANANA WITH APRICOT CARAMEL TRIFLE

EVERYONE LOVES TRIFLE BUT IT DOESN'T NEED TO BE ALCOHOLIC TO BE DELICIOUS. GINGER CAKE MAKES A BRILLIANT BASE, BUT YOU COULD USE YOUR FAMILY'S FAVOURITE FLAVOUR, IF YOU PREFER. TOP WITH PLENTY OF WHIPPED CREAM.

SERVES SIX TO EIGHT

INGREDIENTS
  300ml/½ pint/1¼ cups milk
  1 vanilla pod (bean)
  45ml/3 tbsp caster (superfine) sugar
  20ml/4 tsp cornflour (cornstarch)
  3 egg yolks
  ¼ packet apricot or tangerine jelly
    (flavoured gelatin)
  60ml/4 tbsp apricot conserve
  175–225g/6–8oz ginger cake, cubed
  3 bananas, sliced, with 1
    reserved for topping
  115g/4oz/½ cup granulated sugar
  300ml/½ pint/1¼ cups double
    (heavy) cream
  a few drops of lemon juice

1 Pour the milk into a small pan. Carefully split the vanilla pod down the middle and scrape the tiny seeds into the pan.

2 Add the vanilla pod to the milk and bring just to the boil over a low heat, then remove the pan from the heat. When the milk has cooled slightly, remove the vanilla pod.

COOK'S TIP
Use whatever cake you prefer in the base of the trifle. Leftover Madeira cake, with its tangy citrus flavour, makes a perfect choice. Choose a jelly and conserve that complement the flavour of your cake: strawberry jelly and raspberry conserve are good with lemon cake, or try lemon jelly and peach conserve with a chocolate sponge cake.

3 Whisk together the sugar, cornflour and eggs until pale and creamy. Whisk in the milk and return the whole mixture to the pan. Heat to simmering point, stirring constantly, and cook gently over a low heat until the custard coats the back of a wooden spoon thickly.

4 Leave to cool, covered tightly with clear film (plastic wrap). Ensure the covering is pressed against the surface of the custard to prevent a skin forming.

5 Put the jelly, apricot conserve and 60ml/4 tbsp water in a small pan and heat gently until the jelly dissolves. Set aside until cool, but not set.

VARIATION
For an adult-only version of this trifle, substitute a plainer sponge cake for the ginger cake. Before pouring the jelly (gelatin) mixture over the cubed cake, moisten the cake with a little apricot brandy and a small glass of dessert wine. If you choose to use a different flavoured jelly and conserve, try a different liqueur or brandy that will complement the flavour of the jelly and conserve.

6 Put the cubed cake in a deep serving bowl or dish and pour on the jelly mixture. Cover with sliced bananas, then the custard. Chill for 1–2 hours.

7 Melt the sugar in a small pan with 60ml/4 tbsp water and, when it has dissolved, cook until it is just turning golden. Immediately pour on to a sheet of foil and leave to harden, then break the caramel into pieces.

8 Whip the cream until it forms soft peaks and spread it over the custard. Chill for at least 2 hours, then top with the remaining sliced banana, dipped into lemon juice, and the cracked caramel pieces.

APPLE AND ROSE PETAL SNOW

THIS IS A LOVELY, LIGHT AND REFRESHING DESSERT, WHICH IS IDEAL TO MAKE WHEN THE ORCHARDS ARE GROANING WITH APPLES. THE ROSE PETALS GIVE A DELICATE FRAGRANCE BUT OTHER EDIBLE PETALS, SUCH AS HONEYSUCKLE, LAVENDER AND GERANIUM, COULD ALSO BE USED.

SERVES FOUR

INGREDIENTS
    2 large cooking apples
    150ml/¼ pint/⅔ cup thick
        apple juice
    30ml/1 tbsp rose water
    2 egg whites
    75g/3oz/generous ⅓ cup caster
        (superfine) sugar, or to taste
    a few rose petals from an
        unsprayed rose
    crisp biscuits (cookies) or brandy
        snaps, to serve

COOK'S TIP
This recipe uses raw egg whites but it can also be made with a cooked meringue mixture instead.

1 Peel and chop the apples and cook with the apple juice until soft. Sieve, add the rose water and leave to cool.

2 Whisk the egg whites until peaking, then gently whisk in the sugar. Gently fold together the apple and egg whites. Stir in most of the rose petals.

3 Spoon the snow into four glasses and chill. Serve topped with the remaining petals and crisp biscuits or brandy snaps.

COOK'S TIP
To make sugared rose petals, brush each petal with beaten egg white, sprinkle with granulated sugar and leave to dry.

MANGO AND TANGERINE SORBET

MANGO MAKES THE EASIEST AND MOST DELICIOUS OF SORBETS. IT DOESN'T NEED A SUGAR SYRUP YET STILL GIVES A MELT-IN-THE-MOUTH CONSISTENCY. IF YOU CAN, USE THE SMALL, YELLOW INDIAN MANGOES; THEIR FLAVOUR IS EXQUISITE AND THEIR FLESH IS AMAZINGLY PERFUMED.

MAKES 450ML/¾ PINT/1¾ CUPS

INGREDIENTS
    4 tangerines
    1 lemon
    90g/3½oz/½ cup caster
        (superfine) sugar
    1 large ripe mango
    3 egg whites
    fresh raspberries to serve

COOK'S TIP
Always treat hot syrups with great care as they can cause bad scalds if splashed on to the skin.

VARIATION
For a more elegant dessert, serve scoops of the sorbet in brandy snap baskets or chocolate cases. Sprinkle with fresh berries, to serve.

1 Squeeze the juice from the tangerines and lemon into a small pan. Stir in the caster sugar.

2 Gently heat the mixture and bring to simmering point, skimming constantly. Still stirring, simmer gently until the mixture begins to turn slightly syrupy, then remove the pan from the heat and leave to cool slightly.

3 Purée the mango in a food processor and stir in the syrup. Whisk the egg whites until holding soft peaks and fold into the mango purée. Freeze, whisking every half hour for 3–4 hours, or churn in an ice-cream machine.

4 Serve the sorbet immediately, or leave it to freeze completely, then allow 15–20 minutes at room temperature before serving with raspberries.

FROZEN GRAND MARNIER SOUFFLÉS

LIGHT AND FLUFFY YET ALMOST ICE CREAM, THESE DELICIOUS SOUFFLÉS ARE PERFECT FOR A SPECIAL DINNER. REDCURRANTS OR OTHER SMALL, SOFT FRUITS MAKE A DELICATE DECORATION.

SERVES EIGHT

INGREDIENTS
  200g/7oz/1 cup sugar
  6 large (US extra large) eggs, separated
  15g/½oz/1 tbsp powdered gelatine
  250ml/8fl oz/1 cup milk
  450ml/¾ pint/scant 2 cups double
    (heavy) cream
  60ml/4 tbsp Grand Marnier

1 Wrap a double collar of greaseproof (waxed) paper around eight dessert glasses or ramekins and tie with string. Whisk together 75g/3oz/generous ⅓ cup of the sugar with the egg yolks, until the yolks are pale. This will take about 5 minutes by hand or about 3 minutes with an electric hand mixer.

2 Soak the gelatine in 45ml/3 tbsp cold water. Heat the milk until almost boiling and pour it on to the yolks, whisking constantly. Return to the pan and stir over a low heat until the custard is thick enough to coat the back of the spoon. Remove from the heat. Stir in the gelatine. Pour the custard into a bowl and leave to cool. Whisk occasionally, until on the point of setting.

3 Put the remaining sugar in a pan with 45ml/3 tbsp water and dissolve it over a low heat. Bring to the boil and boil rapidly until it reaches the soft ball stage or 119°C/238°F on a sugar thermometer. Remove from the heat. In a clean bowl, whisk the egg whites until stiff. Pour the hot syrup on to the whites, whisking constantly. Leave to cool.

COOK'S TIP
The soft ball stage of a syrup is when a teaspoon of the mixture dropped into a glass of cold water sets into a ball.

VARIATION
If you like, you can make a single, large dessert in a large soufflé dish, rather than eight individual ones.

4 Add the Grand Marnier to the cold custard. Whisk the cream until it holds soft peaks and fold into the cooled meringue, with the custard. Pour into the prepared glasses or dishes. Freeze overnight. Remove the paper collars and leave at room temperature for 15 minutes before serving.

ICED MOUSSE WITH HOT PINEAPPLE

THIS HEAVENLY COMBINATION OF COCONUT AND PINEAPPLE WILL CONJURE UP THOUGHTS OF SUN, SEA, SAND AND TROPICAL ISLANDS. IF YOU PREFER, REPLACE THE LIQUEUR WITH FRESH ORANGE JUICE.

SERVES SIX TO EIGHT

INGREDIENTS

  4 large (US extra large) eggs
  2.5ml/½ tsp vanilla essence (extract)
  75g/3oz/generous ⅓ cup caster
    (superfine) sugar
  175ml/6fl oz/¾ cup milk
  90ml/6 tbsp coconut milk
  1½ sachets powdered gelatine
  90ml/6 tbsp coconut liqueur
  275ml/9fl oz/generous 1 cup double
    (heavy) cream
  115g/4oz fresh pineapple, grated,
    juice retained
  90–105ml/6–7 tbsp pineapple jam
  50g/2oz shredded coconut, toasted
  a few pieces of pineapple, to decorate

1 Wrap a greaseproof (waxed) paper collar around a 1.2 litre/2 pint/5 cup soufflé dish (see Cook's Tip).

2 Separate the eggs. Beat the yolks with the vanilla and sugar. Bring the milk and coconut milk to the boil, pour over the yolk mixture, whisking constantly, and return to the pan. Continue whisking over a medium heat until the custard coats the back of a wooden spoon. Sprinkle on the gelatine, leave for 20 seconds, then stir until dissolved.

COOK'S TIP
To make a dish collar, cut a piece of greaseproof (waxed) paper the length of the circumference of the dish and about 20cm/8in wide. Fold lengthways, attach one end at the rim of the dish with sticky tape, wrap it tightly around the dish and fasten the other end with tape.

3 Stir the liqueur into the custard, then place the pan in a bowl of ice to chill. Whip the cream until it stands in peaks and, in another bowl, whisk the egg whites to soft peaks. Fold them both carefully and evenly into the custard. Spoon into the prepared soufflé dish and leave to set for 2 hours. Freeze the mousse for 2–3 hours before serving.

4 Heat the pineapple and jam in a small pan with 30–45ml/2–3 tbsp water and simmer for 2–3 minutes until really hot. To serve, remove the paper collar from the soufflé and carefully press the toasted coconut against the sides. Decorate the top with more pieces of fresh pineapple and serve immediately with the hot sauce.

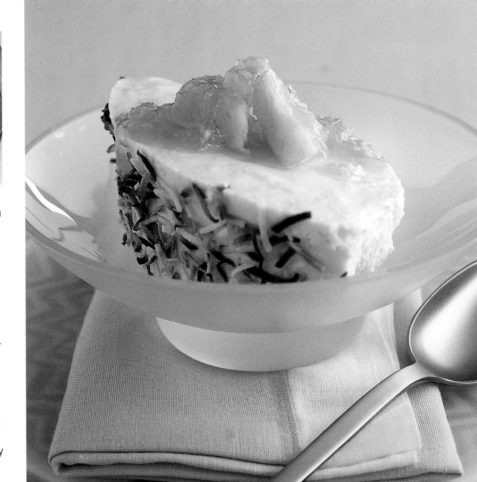

RICH VANILLA ICE CREAM

This classic vanilla ice cream is quite superb. Serve it on its own or use as the base for other ices and desserts.

MAKES 750ML/1¼ PINTS/3 CUPS

INGREDIENTS
    300ml/½ pint/1¼ cups single
        (light) cream
    1 vanilla pod (bean)
    3 egg yolks
    45ml/3 tbsp caster (superfine) sugar
    10ml/2 tsp cornflour (cornstarch)
    300ml/½ pint/1¼ cups double
        (heavy) cream, whipped

VARIATION
Add 175g/6oz melted plain (semisweet) chocolate and 30ml/2 tbsp (unsweetened) cocoa powder when making the custard.

1 Put the cream in a small pan. Split the vanilla pod and scrape out the tiny seeds. Add them to the cream with the pod. Bring the cream just to the boil, then turn off the heat.

2 Whisk together the eggs, sugar and cornflour until pale and creamy. Remove the vanilla pod from the cream and whisk into the egg mixture. Return the mixture to the pan and bring to a simmer, stirring constantly. Cook gently until the custard coats the back of a wooden spoon.

3 Leave the custard to cool completely, then whisk well and fold in the whipped cream. Spoon it into a freezer container and freeze, whisking once every hour for 2–3 hours, or churn in an ice-cream maker until almost frozen, then transfer to the freezer.

ICED RASPBERRY PAVLOVA ROULADE

THIS MELT-IN-THE-MOUTH MERINGUE, ROLLED AROUND VANILLA CREAM AND LUSCIOUS RASPBERRIES, IS A STAR DINNER-PARTY ATTRACTION, AND IS SURPRISINGLY QUICK AND SIMPLE TO MAKE.

SERVES SIX TO EIGHT

INGREDIENTS
10ml/2 tsp cornflour (cornstarch)
225g/8oz/generous 1 cup caster (superfine) sugar
4 egg whites, at room temperature
icing (confectioners') sugar, sifted
300ml/½ pint/1¼ cups double (heavy) cream or whipping cream
drops of vanilla essence (extract)
175g/6oz/1 cup raspberries, partly frozen, plus extra to serve

1 Line a 33 × 23cm/13 × 9in Swiss-roll tin (jelly-roll pan) with baking parchment. Sift the cornflour into a bowl and blend evenly with the sugar.

2 Using a balloon whisk or hand-held electric beaters, whisk the egg whites in a clean mixing bowl until they form stiff peaks, but are not dry and crumbly.

3 Gradually whisk in the caster sugar, a few spoonfuls at a time, until the mixture becomes stiff and glossy.

4 Spoon the mixture into the prepared tin and flatten the top. Place in a cold oven and turn it to 150°C/300°F/Gas 2. Cook for 1 hour until the top is crisp and the meringue still feels springy (if it appears to be colouring too early while cooking, reduce the temperature).

5 Turn out on to a double sheet of greaseproof (waxed) paper sprinkled with sifted icing sugar and leave to cool.

6 Meanwhile, whip the cream with the vanilla essence and stir in the partly frozen raspberries. Freeze the mixture until required.

7 When the meringue has cooled, carefully spread the cream over it, then roll up, using the paper as a support. Freeze for about 1 hour before serving, sprinkled with more icing sugar and extra raspberries.

COOK'S TIP
The filling can be as varied as you wish. Try flavouring the cream with liqueur or home-made lemon curd, or fill with softened ice cream, then return the roulade to the freezer immediately.

CHOCOLATE CHESTNUT ROULADE

THIS COMBINATION OF INTENSE FLAVOURS PRODUCES A VERY RICH DESSERT, SO SERVE IT WELL CHILLED AND IN THIN SLICES. IT CAN BE SLICED MORE EASILY WHEN IT IS VERY COLD.

SERVES TEN TO TWELVE

INGREDIENTS
  oil, for greasing
  175g/6oz dark (bittersweet)
    chocolate, chopped
  30ml/2 tbsp (unsweetened) cocoa
    powder, sifted, plus extra
  50ml/2fl oz/¼ cup strong coffee
  6 eggs, separated
  75g/3oz/6 tbsp caster
    (superfine) sugar
  pinch of cream of tartar
  5ml/1 tsp vanilla essence (extract)
  glacé (candied) chestnuts, to decorate
For the filling
  475ml/16fl oz/2 cups double
    (heavy) cream
  30ml/2 tbsp coffee-flavoured liqueur
  350g/12oz can chestnut purée
  115g/4oz dark chocolate, grated
  thick cream, to serve

1 Preheat the oven to 180°C/350°F/ Gas 4. Grease the base and sides of a 39 × 27 × 2.5cm/15½ × 10½ × 1in Swiss-roll tin (jelly-roll pan). Line with baking parchment, allowing a 2.5cm/ 1in overhang.

2 Melt the chocolate in the top of a double boiler over a low heat, stirring frequently. Set aside. Dissolve the cocoa in the freshly brewed coffee. Stir to make a smooth paste. Set aside.

COOK'S TIP
Beating egg whites should always be the last step in the preparation of cake mixtures. Once they are beaten, they should be folded in immediately.

3 With an electric mixer or in a bowl using a whisk, beat the egg yolks with half the sugar for about 3–5 minutes until pale and thick. Slowly beat in the melted chocolate and cocoa-coffee paste until just blended.

4 In another bowl, beat the egg whites and cream of tartar until stiff peaks form. Sprinkle the remaining sugar over in two batches and beat until stiff and glossy, then beat in the vanilla.

5 Stir a spoonful of the whisked whites into the chocolate mixture to lighten it, then fold in the remainder.

6 Spoon the mixture into the tin and level the top. Bake for 20–25 minutes or until the cake springs back when lightly pressed with the fingertips.

7 Meanwhile, dust a clean dishtowel with the extra cocoa powder. As soon as the cake is cooked, carefully turn it out on to the dishtowel and gently peel off the lining paper from the base. Starting at a narrow end, roll the cake and the dishtowel together Swiss-roll fashion. Cool completely.

8 To make the filling, whip the cream and liqueur until soft peaks form. Beat a spoonful of cream into the chestnut purée to lighten it, then fold in the remaining cream and most of the grated chocolate. Reserve a quarter of the chestnut cream mixture.

9 To assemble the roulade, unroll the cake and spread with the filling, to within 2.5cm/1in of the edges. Gently roll it up, using the dishtowel for support.

10 Place the roulade, seam side down, on a serving plate. Spoon the reserved chestnut cream into a small icing (pastry) bag and pipe rosettes along the top. Dust with cocoa and decorate with glacé chestnuts and grated chocolate.

HOT
DESSERTS

There is nothing better than a hot dessert at the end of a meal. The classic French butter pudding, Black Cherry Clafoutis, or a wonderful steamed Chocolate Pudding with Rum Custard are great on a cold winter evening. Warm and fluffy Zabaglione, and Grilled Peaches with Meringues offer a lighter, yet equally tempting, alternative. Children love hot desserts, too, and this chapter includes a whole range of recipes that are sure to be popular with the whole family. Apricot Panettone Pudding provides a twist on the traditional bread and butter pudding, and Rhubarb Meringue Pie combines the sharp, tangy flavour of rhubarb with mouthwatering meringue and crisp pastry.

GRILLED PEACHES ᵂᴵᵀᴴ MERINGUES

ALTHOUGH RIPE PEACHES NEED LITTLE TO SET THEM OFF, THESE MINI MERINGUES, MADE WITH BROWN SUGAR, MAKE A PERFECT ACCOMPANIMENT FOR THE SWEET GRILLED PEACHES.

SERVES SIX

INGREDIENTS
  2 egg whites
  115g/4oz/½ cup soft light brown
    sugar, reserving 5ml/1 tsp for
    the peaches
  pinch of ground cinnamon
  6 ripe peaches, or nectarines
  15–30ml/1–2 tbsp orange juice
  5ml/1 tsp finely grated orange rind,
    to serve
  crème fraîche, to serve

COOK'S TIP
Use leftover egg whites to make these little cinnamon-flavoured meringues. The meringues can be stored in an airtight container for about 2 weeks. Serve them after dinner with coffee or with desserts in place of biscuits (cookies).

1 Preheat the oven to 140°C/275°F/ Gas 1. Line two large baking trays with non-stick baking parchment.

2 Whisk the egg whites until they form stiff peaks. Gradually whisk in the sugar and ground cinnamon until the mixture is stiff and glossy. Pipe 18 very small meringues on to the trays and bake for 40 minutes. Leave in the oven to cool.

3 Meanwhile, halve and stone (pit) the peaches. Brush the cut sides of the fruit with orange juice and sprinkle on a little sugar. Grill (broil) for 4–5 minutes until just beginning to caramelize.

4 Stir the orange rind into the crème fraîche with 15ml/1 tbsp orange juice. Serve the peaches topped with a little crème fraîche and three meringues.

ZABAGLIONE

LIGHT AS AIR AND WONDERFULLY ALCOHOLIC, THIS WARM EGG CUSTARD IS A MUCH-LOVED ITALIAN DESSERT. THOUGH TRADITIONALLY MADE WITH MARSALA, THIS FORTIFIED WINE CAN BE REPLACED BY MADEIRA OR SWEET SHERRY.

2 Gradually add the Marsala, Madeira or sherry to the egg mixture, 15ml/ 1 tbsp at a time, whisking well after each addition.

3 Place the bowl over a pan of gently simmering water and continue to whisk for 5–7 minutes, until the mixture becomes thick; when the beaters are lifted they should leave a thick trail on the surface of the mixture. Do not be tempted to underbeat the mixture, as the zabaglione will be too runny and will be likely to separate.

4 Pour into four warmed, stemmed glasses and serve immediately with amaretti for dipping.

SERVES FOUR

INGREDIENTS
    4 egg yolks
    50g/2oz/¼ cup caster
      (superfine) sugar
    60ml/4 tbsp Marsala, Madeira
      or sweet sherry
    amaretti, to serve

VARIATION
To make a chocolate zabaglione, whisk in 30ml/2 tbsp unsweetened cocoa powder with the wine or sherry and serve dusted with cocoa powder.

1 Place the egg yolks and sugar in a large heatproof bowl, and whisk with an electric beater until the mixture is pale and thick.

COOK'S TIP
Zabaglione is also delicious served as a sauce with cooked fruit desserts. Try serving it with poached pears, grilled (broiled) peaches or baked bananas to create a really special dessert.

FRUIT-FILLED SOUFFLÉ OMELETTE

THIS IMPRESSIVE DISH IS SURPRISINGLY QUICK AND EASY TO MAKE. THE CREAMY OMELETTE FLUFFS UP IN THE PAN, FLOPS OVER TO ENVELOP ITS FILLING OF FRUITS IN LIQUEUR AND THEN SLIDES GRACEFULLY ON TO THE PLATE.

SERVES TWO

INGREDIENTS

   75g/3oz/¾ cup strawberries, hulled
   45ml/3 tbsp kirsch, brandy
    or Cointreau
   3 eggs, separated
   30ml/2 tbsp caster (superfine) sugar
   45ml/3 tbsp double (heavy)
    cream, whipped
   a few drops of vanilla
    essence (extract)
   25g/1oz/2 tbsp butter
   icing (confectioners') sugar, sifted

3 Melt the butter in an omelette pan. When sizzling, pour in the egg mixture and cook until set underneath, shaking occasionally. Spoon on the strawberries and liqueur and, tilting the pan, slide the omelette so that it folds over.

4 Carefully slide the omelette on to a warm serving plate, spoon over the remaining liqueur, and serve dredged with icing sugar. Cut the omelette in half, transfer to two warmed plates and eat immediately.

1 Cut the strawberries in half and place in a bowl. Pour over 30ml/2 tbsp of the liqueur and set aside to marinate.

2 Beat the egg yolks and sugar together until pale and fluffy, then fold in the whipped cream and vanilla essence. Whisk the egg whites in a very large, grease-free bowl until stiff, then carefully fold in the yolks.

COOK'S TIP
You can give your omelette a professional look by marking sizzling grill lines on top. Protecting your hand with an oven glove, hold a long, wooden-handled skewer directly over a gas flame until it becomes very hot and changes colour. Sprinkle the top of the omelette with icing sugar, then place the hot skewer on the sugar, which will caramelize very quickly. Working quickly, before the skewer becomes too cold to caramelize the sugar, make as many lines as you like.

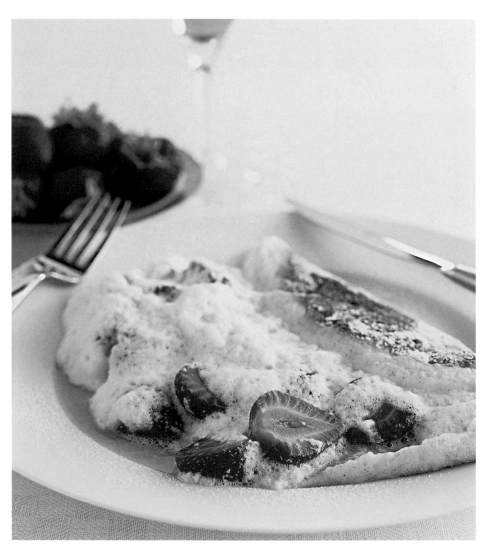

PINEAPPLE BAKED ALASKA

MOST CHILDREN LOVE THE SURPRISE OF THIS CLASSIC DESSERT — HOT MERINGUE WITH ICE-COLD ICE CREAM INSIDE. HERE'S A NEW VARIATION TO TRY OUT ON THEM.

SERVES THREE TO FOUR

INGREDIENTS

   3 large (US extra large) egg whites
   150g/5oz/¾ cup sugar
   25g/1oz desiccated (dry unsweetened shredded) coconut
   175–225g/6–8oz piece ginger or chocolate cake
   6 slices ripe, peeled pineapple
   500ml/17fl oz/2¼ cups vanilla ice cream, in a brick
   a few cherries or figs, to decorate

1 Preheat the oven to 230°C/450°F/ Gas 8. Whisk the egg whites in a grease-free bowl until stiff, then whisk in the sugar until the mixture is stiff and glossy. Fold in the coconut.

2 Slice the cake into two thick layers the same rectangular shape as the ice cream. Cut the pineapple into triangles or quarters, cutting it over the cake to catch any drips. On a baking tray, arrange the fruit on top of one slice of cake. Top with the ice cream and then the second layer of cake.

3 Spread the meringue over the cake and ice cream, and bake in the oven for 5–7 minutes, or until turning golden. Serve immediately, topped with fruit.

COOK'S TIP
Do not use soft-scoop ice cream for this dessert as it will soften too quickly.

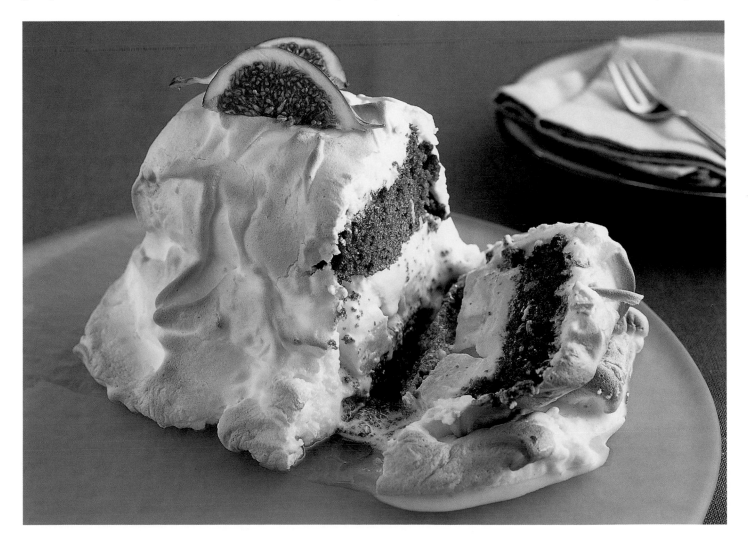

HOT CHOCOLATE SOUFFLÉS

THESE RICH, INDIVIDUAL SOUFFLÉS HAVE THE MEREST HINT OF ORANGE IN THEM, AND ARE DIVINE WITH THE WHITE CHOCOLATE SAUCE POURED INTO THE MIDDLE.

SERVES SIX

INGREDIENTS
   butter, for greasing
   45ml/3 tbsp caster (superfine) sugar
   175g/6oz plain (semisweet)
     chocolate, chopped
   150g/5oz/⅔ cup unsalted (sweet)
     butter, cut in small pieces
   4 large (US extra large) eggs
   1.5ml/¼ tsp cream of tartar
   icing (confectioners') sugar,
     for dusting
For the sauce
   75g/3oz white chocolate, chopped
   90ml/6 tbsp whipping cream
   15–30ml/1–2 tbsp orange liqueur
   grated rind of ½ orange

1 Generously butter six 150ml/¼ pint/ ⅔ cup ramekins. Sprinkle each with a little caster sugar and tap out any excess. Place the ramekins on a baking sheet.

2 Melt the chocolate and butter in a bowl placed over a pan of simmering water, stirring. Remove the bowl from the heat and cool slightly. Separate the eggs and set the whites aside. Beat the yolks into the chocolate mixture. Set aside, stirring occasionally.

3 Preheat the oven to 220°C/425°F/ Gas 7. In a large, grease-free bowl, whisk the egg whites slowly until frothy. Add the cream of tartar, increase the speed and whisk until the whites form soft peaks. Gradually sprinkle over the caster sugar, 15ml/1 tbsp at a time, whisking until the whites become stiff and glossy.

4 Stir a third of the whites into the cooled chocolate mixture to lighten it, then pour the mixture over the remaining whites.

5 Using a rubber spatula or large metal spoon, gently fold the sauce into the whites, cutting down to the bottom, then along the sides and up to the top in a semicircular motion until the chocolate mixture and egg whites are just combined; don't worry about a few white streaks. Spoon the combined mixture into the prepared dishes.

VARIATION
Like orange, coffee complements the flavour of chocolate perfectly. Try using a coffee liqueur, such as Kahlúa or Tia Maria, instead of the orange liqueur in the soufflé mixture and sauce.

6 To make the sauce, put the chopped chocolate and the cream into a small pan. Place over a very low heat and warm, stirring constantly until melted and smooth. Remove the pan from the heat and stir in the liqueur and orange rind, then pour into a serving jug (pitcher) and keep warm.

7 Bake the soufflés in the preheated oven for 10–12 minutes until risen and set, but still slightly wobbly in the centre. Dust with icing sugar and serve immediately with the warm white chocolate sauce.

COOK'S TIP
These soufflés are ideal for serving at a dinner party because they can be prepared in advance, ready for baking at the last minute. Follow steps 1–5 above, then tightly cover the uncooked soufflés with clear film (plastic wrap). Set aside in a cool, but not cold, place until ready to cook. If the soufflés become too cold while waiting to be cooked, allow an extra 2–3 minutes cooking time.

CHOCOLATE PUDDING WITH RUM CUSTARD

WITH MELTING MOMENTS OF CHOCOLATE IN EVERY MOUTHFUL, THESE LITTLE PUDDINGS WON'T LAST LONG. THE RUM CUSTARD TURNS THEM INTO A MORE ADULT PUDDING; FOR A FAMILY DESSERT, FLAVOUR THE CUSTARD WITH VANILLA OR ORANGE RIND INSTEAD.

SERVES SIX

INGREDIENTS
    115g/4oz/½ cup butter, plus extra
    115g/4oz/½ cup soft light
      brown sugar
    2 eggs, beaten
    a few drops of vanilla
      essence (extract)
    45ml/3 tbsp cocoa powder, sieved
    115g/4oz/1 cup self-raising (self-
      rising) flour
    75g/3oz bitter chocolate, chopped
    a little milk, warmed
For the custard
    250ml/8fl oz/1 cup milk
    15ml/1 tbsp caster (superfine) sugar
    2 egg yolks
    10ml/2 tsp cornflour (cornstarch)
    30–45ml/2–3 tbsp rum

1 Lightly grease six individual dariole moulds. Cream the butter and sugar until pale and creamy. Gently blend in the eggs and the vanilla essence.

2 Sift together the cocoa and flour, and fold gently into the egg mixture with the chopped chocolate and sufficient milk to give a soft dropping consistency.

COOK'S TIP
To microwave the pudding, spoon the mixture into a microwave-proof bowl (at least 300ml/½ pint/1¼ cups larger than necessary). Cover loosely with clear film (plastic wrap) and microwave on full power for about 5 minutes, depending on the power of your machine. Leave to stand for 5 minutes before serving.

3 Spoon the mixture into the basin or moulds, cover with buttered greaseproof (waxed) paper and tie down. Fill a pan with 2.5–5cm/1–2in water, place the puddings in the pan, cover with a lid and bring to the boil. Steam the large pudding for 1½–2 hours and the individual puddings for 45–50 minutes, topping up with water if necessary. When firm, turn out on to warm plates.

4 To make the rum custard, bring the milk and sugar to the boil. Whisk together the egg yolks and cornflour, then pour on the hot milk, whisking constantly. Return the mixture to the pan and stir while it slowly comes back to the boil. Allow the sauce to simmer gently as it thickens, stirring. Remove from the heat, stir in the rum and pour over the puddings. Serve immediately.

APRICOT PANETTONE PUDDING

THE COMBINATION OF THE LIGHT ITALIAN FRUIT BREAD, APRICOTS AND PECAN NUTS PRODUCES A WONDERFULLY RICH VERSION OF TRADITIONAL BREAD-AND-BUTTER PUDDING.

2 Pour the milk into a small pan and add the vanilla essence. Warm the milk over a medium heat until it just barely simmers. In a large bowl, mix together the beaten egg and maple syrup, grate in the nutmeg, then whisk in the hot milk.

3 Preheat the oven to 200°C/400°F/ Gas 6. Pour the milk mixture over the panettone, lightly pressing down each slice so that it is totally submerged in the mixture. Set the dish aside and leave the pudding to stand for at least 10 minutes.

4 Scatter the reserved pecan nuts over the top and sprinkle with the demerara sugar and nutmeg. Bake for about 40 minutes until risen and golden.

SERVES SIX

INGREDIENTS
    unsalted butter, for greasing
    350g/12oz panettone, sliced
      into triangles
    25g/1oz/¼ cup pecan nuts
    75g/3oz/⅓ cup ready-to-eat dried
      apricots, chopped
    500ml/17fl oz/2¼ cups semi-
      skimmed (low-fat) milk
    5ml/1 tsp vanilla essence (extract)
    1 large (US extra large) egg, beaten
    30ml/2 tbsp maple syrup
    2.5ml/½ tsp grated nutmeg, plus
      extra for sprinkling
    demerara (raw) sugar, for sprinkling

1 Grease a 1 litre/1¾ pint/4 cup baking dish. Arrange half the panettone in the base of the dish, scatter over half the pecan nuts and all the dried apricots, then add another layer of panettone on top, spreading it as evenly as you can.

COOK'S TIP
Panettone is a sweet Italian yeast bread made with raisins, citron, pine nuts and star anise. It is traditionally served at Christmas and is easier to obtain at that time of year. If it is not available, use any sweet yeasted fruit loaf instead.

RHUBARB MERINGUE PIE

*THE SHARP TANG OF RHUBARB WITH ITS SWEET MERINGUE TOPPING WILL REALLY TANTALIZE THE
TASTE BUDS. THIS DESSERT IS DELICIOUS HOT OR COLD WITH CREAM OR VANILLA ICE CREAM.*

3 Meanwhile, put the rhubarb, 75g/3oz/
6 tbsp of the remaining sugar and the
orange rind in a pan. Cover with a lid
and cook over a low heat until the
rhubarb is tender.

4 Remove the beans and paper from the
pastry case, then brush all over with a
little of the remaining egg yolk. Bake for
10–15 minutes, until the pastry is crisp.

5 Blend together the cornflour and the
orange juice in a small bowl. Off the
heat, stir the cornflour mixture into the
cooked rhubarb, then bring to the boil,
stirring constantly until thickened. Cook
for a further 1–2 minutes. Cool slightly,
then beat in the remaining egg yolks.
Pour into the flan case.

6 Whisk the egg whites until they form
soft peaks, then whisk in the remaining
sugar, 15ml/1 tbsp at a time, whisking
well after each addition.

SERVES SIX

INGREDIENTS
  200g/7oz/1¾ cups plain (all-purpose)
    flour, plus extra for flouring
  25g/1oz/⅓ cup ground walnuts
  115g/4oz/½ cup butter, diced
  275g/10oz/generous 1½ cups
    caster (superfine) sugar
  4 egg yolks
  675g/1½ lb rhubarb, cut into
    small pieces
  finely grated rind and juice of
    3 blood or navel oranges
  75ml/5 tbsp cornflour (cornstarch)
  3 egg whites
  whipped cream, to serve

1 Sift the flour into a bowl and add the
ground walnuts. Rub in the butter until
the mixture resembles very fine breadcrumbs. Stir in 30ml/2 tbsp of the sugar
with 1 egg yolk beaten with 15ml/1 tbsp
water. Mix to a firm dough. Turn out on
to a floured surface and knead lightly.
Wrap in a plastic bag and chill for at
least 30 minutes.

2 Preheat the oven to 190°C/375°F/
Gas 5. Roll out the pastry on a lightly
floured surface and use to line a 23cm/
9in fluted flan tin (quiche pan). Prick
the base with a fork. Line the pastry
with baking parchment and fill with
baking beans. Bake for 15 minutes.

7 Swirl the meringue over the filling to
cover completely. Bake for 25 minutes
until golden. Serve warm, or leave to
cool for about 30 minutes and serve,
with whipped cream.

BLACK CHERRY CLAFOUTIS

CLAFOUTIS IS A BATTER PUDDING THAT ORIGINATED IN THE LIMOUSIN AREA OF CENTRAL FRANCE. IT IS OFTEN MADE WITH CREAM AND TRADITIONALLY USES SLIGHTLY TART BLACK CHERRIES, ALTHOUGH OTHER SOFT FRUITS CAN ALSO GIVE DELICIOUS RESULTS.

SERVES SIX

INGREDIENTS
 butter, for greasing
 450g/1lb/2 cups black
  cherries, pitted
 25g/1oz/¼ cup plain
  (all-purpose) flour
 50g/2oz/½ cup icing (confectioners')
  sugar, plus extra for dusting
 4 eggs, beaten
 250ml/8fl oz/1 cup full-cream
  (whole) milk
 30ml/2 tbsp cherry liqueur

1 Preheat the oven to 180°C/350°F/ Gas 4. Generously grease a 1.2 litre/ 2 pint/5 cup dish and add the cherries.

2 Sift the flour and icing sugar into a large mixing bowl, then gradually whisk in the beaten eggs until the mixture is smooth. Whisk in the milk until well blended, then stir in the liqueur.

3 Pour the batter into the baking dish. Transfer to the oven and bake for about 40 minutes, or until just set and light golden brown. Insert a knife into the centre of the pudding to test if it is cooked in the middle; the blade should come out clean.

4 Allow the pudding to cool for at least 15 minutes. Dust liberally with icing sugar just before serving, either warm or at room temperature.

VARIATIONS
Try other liqueurs in this dessert. Almond-flavoured liqueur is delicious teamed with cherries, while hazelnut, raspberry or orange liqueurs will also work well. Other fruits that can be used in this pudding include blackberries, blueberries, plums and apricots.

PRUNE TART WITH CUSTARD FILLING

PRUNES AND ARMAGNAC MAKE A FANTASTIC COMBINATION BUT, IF YOU PREFER, REPLACE THE LIQUEUR WITH FRESH ORANGE JUICE.

3 Turn out on a clean, lightly floured surface and bring the mixture together into a ball. Leave for 10 minutes to rest.

4 Flour a 28 x 18cm/11 x 7in loose-bottomed tin (pan). Roll out the pastry and line the tin; don't worry if you have to push it into shape, as this pastry is easy to mould. Chill for 10–20 minutes.

5 Line the pastry case with baking parchment, fill with baking beans, then bake for 15 minutes. Remove the paper and beans, and bake for 12 minutes. Brush the pastry base with the reserved egg white while it is still hot. Set aside to cool slightly.

6 Bring the milk and vanilla essence to the boil. In a bowl, whisk the egg yolks and 40g/1½oz/3 tbsp sugar until thick, pale and fluffy, then whisk in the cornflour. Strain in the milk and whisk until there are no lumps.

SERVES SIX TO EIGHT

INGREDIENTS
  225g/8oz/1 cup pitted prunes
  50ml/2fl oz/¼ cup brandy
  175g/6oz/1½ cups plain (all-purpose)
    flour, sifted, plus extra for dusting
  pinch of salt
  90g/3½oz/scant ½ cup sugar
  115g/4oz/½ cup unsalted
    (sweet) butter
  1 egg, plus 4 egg yolks
  300ml/½ pint/1¼ cups milk
  a few drops of vanilla
    essence (extract)
  15g/½oz/2 tbsp cornflour
    (cornstarch)
  25g/1oz/¼ cup flaked
    (sliced) almonds
  icing (confectioners') sugar, sifted

1 Place the prunes in a mixing bowl and pour over the brandy. Leave in a warm place to soak.

2 Preheat the oven to 200°C/400°F/ Gas 6. Place the flour, salt, 50g/2oz/ ¼ cup sugar, butter and egg, reserving 5ml/1 tsp egg white, in a food processor and process until blended.

7 Return to the pan and bring to the boil, whisking all the time to remove any lumps. Cook for about 2 minutes until thick and smooth, then set aside to cool. Press clear film (plastic wrap) on to the surface of the custard.

8 Stir any prune liquid into the custard, then spread over the pastry case. Arrange the prunes on top, sprinkle with the flaked almonds and icing sugar, and return to the oven for 10 minutes until golden and glazed. Remove from the oven and leave to cool. Serve hot or at room temperature.

CUSTARD TART WITH PLUMS

WHEN THIS TART IS MADE WITH REALLY RIPE, SWEET PLUMS, IT MAKES A WONDERFUL HOT OR COLD WEEKEND DESSERT. IT IS DELICIOUS SERVED WITH THICK CREAM OR ICE CREAM.

2 Flour a deep 18cm/7in square or 20cm/8in round loose-bottomed tin (pan). Roll out the pastry and use to line the tin. This pastry is soft at this stage, so don't worry if you have to push it into shape. Chill for 20 minutes.

3 Preheat the oven to 200°C/400°F/ Gas 6. Line the pastry with baking parchment and fill with baking beans, then bake for 15 minutes. Remove the parchment paper and beans, reduce the heat to 180°C/350°F/Gas 4 and bake for about 5 minutes more until the base is dry.

SERVES FOUR TO SIX

INGREDIENTS
175g/6oz/1½ cups flour, sifted
pinch of salt
45ml/3 tbsp caster (superfine) sugar
115g/4oz/½ cup unsalted butter
2 eggs, plus 2 yolks
350g/12oz ripe plums
300ml/½ pint/1¼ cups milk
few drops of vanilla essence (extract)
thick cream or ice cream, to serve
flaked (sliced) almonds and icing
  (confectioners') sugar, to decorate

1 Place the flour, salt, 15ml/1 tbsp of the sugar, the butter and one of the eggs in a food processor or blender and process until thoroughly combined. Turn out the mixture on to a clean, lightly floured surface and bring it together into a ball. Cover the pastry and leave for 10 minutes to rest.

VARIATIONS
This tart is equally delicious made with apricots, peaches or nectarines. Make a nutty pastry by replacing 15ml/1 tbsp of the flour with ground almonds.

4 Halve and stone (pit) the plums, and arrange them neatly in the pastry case. Whisk together the remaining egg and egg yolks with the sugar, the milk and vanilla essence and pour over the fruit.

5 Return the tart to the oven and bake for 25–30 minutes. When the custard is just firm to the touch, remove the tart from the oven and allow to cool slightly. Sprinkle with flaked almonds and dredge with icing sugar before serving. Add a generous dollop of cream or ice cream to each portion.

COOKIES, CAKES AND BREADS

Eggs are an essential ingredient for crisp cookies, light and fluffy sponges, moist fruit cakes and rich breads. Eggs produce wonderfully tempting cookies, such as Cinnamon and Orange Tuiles and Oaty Chocolate-chip Cookies, and help the classic whisked sponge used in Fresh Fruit Genoese Sponge to rise beautifully, giving it an incredibly light texture. Frosted Carrot and Parsnip Cake uses not only eggs in the deliciously moist crumb, but also lightly cooked whisked egg whites for the mouthwatering meringue topping. Whole eggs are used to enrich breads, such as Honey and Saffron Bread, while eggs with dyed bright red shells are used to decorate the traditional Greek Easter Egg Bread.

OATY CHOCOLATE-CHIP COOKIES

THESE CRUNCHY COOKIES ARE EASY ENOUGH FOR CHILDREN TO MAKE BY THEMSELVES AND ARE SURE TO DISAPPEAR AS SOON AS THEY ARE PUT ON THE TABLE.

MAKES ABOUT TWENTY

INGREDIENTS
 115g/4oz/½ cup butter or
   soft margarine, plus extra
   for greasing
 115g/4oz/½ cup soft
   dark brown sugar
 2 eggs, lightly beaten
 45–60ml/3–4 tbsp milk
 5ml/1 tsp vanilla essence (extract)
 150g/5oz/1¼ cups plain
   (all-purpose) flour
 5ml/1 tsp baking powder
 pinch of salt
 115g/4oz/generous 1 cup rolled oats
 175g/6oz plain (semisweet)
   chocolate chips
 115g/4oz/1 cup pecan
   nuts, chopped

1 Cream the butter, or margarine, and sugar in a large bowl until pale and fluffy. Add the beaten eggs, milk and vanilla essence, and beat thoroughly.

2 Sift in the flour, baking powder and salt, and stir in until well mixed. Fold in the rolled oats, chocolate chips and chopped pecan nuts.

3 Chill the mixture for at least 1 hour. Preheat the oven to 180°C/350°F/Gas 4. Grease two large baking trays.

4 Using two teaspoons, place mounds well apart on the trays and flatten with a spoon or fork. Bake for 10–12 minutes until the edges are just colouring, then cool on wire racks.

CHOCOLATE TRUFFLES

THESE IRRESISTIBLE AFTER-DINNER TRUFFLES MELT IN THE MOUTH. USE A GOOD-QUALITY CHOCOLATE WITH A HIGH PERCENTAGE OF COCOA SOLIDS TO GIVE A REAL DEPTH OF FLAVOUR.

MAKES TWENTY TO THIRTY

INGREDIENTS
 175ml/6fl oz/¾ cup double
  (heavy) cream
 1 egg yolk, beaten
 275g/10oz plain (semisweet)
  Belgian chocolate, chopped
 25g/1oz/2 tbsp unsalted (sweet)
  butter, cut into pieces
 30–45ml/2–3 tbsp brandy
  (optional)
For the coatings
 cocoa powder
 finely chopped pistachio nuts
  or hazelnuts
 400g/14oz plain, milk or white
  chocolate, or a mixture

1 Bring the cream to the boil, then remove the pan from the heat and beat in the egg yolk. Add the chocolate, then stir until melted and smooth. Stir in the butter and the brandy, if using, then strain into a bowl and leave to cool. Cover and chill for 6–8 hours.

2 Line a baking sheet with greaseproof (waxed) paper. Using two teaspoons, shape the chilled chocolate mixture into 20–30 balls and place on the prepared paper. Rechill the chocolate mixture if it becomes too soft.

3 To coat the truffles with cocoa, sift some powder into a small bowl, drop in the truffles, one at a time, and roll to coat well. To coat them with nuts, roll the truffles in finely chopped pistachio nuts or hazelnuts.

4 To coat with chocolate, freeze the truffles for at least 1 hour. In a small bowl, melt the plain, milk or white chocolate over a pan of barely simmering water, stirring until melted and smooth, then allow to cool slightly.

5 Using a fork, dip the frozen truffles into the cooled chocolate, one at a time, tapping the fork on the edge of the bowl to shake off the excess. Place on a baking sheet lined with non-stick baking parchment and chill. If the chocolate thickens, reheat until smooth. All the truffles can be stored, well wrapped, in the refrigerator for up to 10 days.

GOLDEN GINGER MACAROONS

*WITH THEIR WARM, SPICY, GINGER FLAVOUR, THESE SLIGHTLY CHEWY LITTLE BISCUITS ARE GOOD
SERVED WITH ICE CREAM AND WILL GO WELL WITH MID-MORNING OR AFTER-DINNER COFFEE.*

MAKES EIGHTEEN TO TWENTY

INGREDIENTS
1 egg white
75g/3oz/scant ½ cup soft
  light brown sugar
115g/4oz/1 cup ground
  almonds
5ml/1 tsp ground ginger

VARIATIONS
You can substitute other ground nuts,
such as hazelnuts or walnuts, for the
almonds. Ground cinnamon or mixed
(apple pie) spice could be added in
place of the ginger.

1 Preheat the oven to 180°C/350°F/
Gas 4. In a large, grease-free bowl,
whisk the egg white until stiff and
standing in peaks, but not crumbly,
then whisk in the brown sugar.

2 Sprinkle the ground almonds and
ginger over the whisked egg white, and
gently fold them together.

3 Using two teaspoons, place spoonfuls
of the mixture on baking trays, leaving
plenty of space between each. Bake for
about 20 minutes until pale golden
brown and just turning crisp.

4 Leave to cool slightly on the baking
trays before transferring to a wire rack
to cool completely.

NUTTY NOUGAT

*THIS CHEWY TREAT IS MADE FROM EGG WHITE WHISKED TOGETHER WITH A HOT SUGAR SYRUP. NUTS
AND CANDIED FRUITS ARE TRADITIONALLY ADDED BUT OTHER FRUITS, SUCH AS DRIED APRICOTS OR
GLACÉ CHERRIES, CAN ALSO BE USED.*

MAKES ABOUT 500G/1½LB

INGREDIENTS
225g/8oz/generous 1 cup sugar
225g/8oz/1 cup clear honey or
  golden (light corn) syrup
1 large (US extra large) egg white
115g/4oz/1 cup flaked (sliced)
  almonds or chopped pistachio
  nuts, roasted

1 Line a 17.5cm/7in square tin with rice
paper and set aside.

COOK'S TIP
If you make this nougat on a very warm
day, you will find it takes longer to firm
up and you will need to wait a little
longer before cutting. It may help to take
it out of the tin as soon as it has set.

2 Place the sugar, clear honey or golden
syrup and 60ml/4 tbsp water in a large
heavy pan and warm over a gentle heat
until the sugar has dissolved totally,
stirring frequently.

3 Bring the syrup to the boil and boil
gently to the soft crack stage, or 151°C/
304°F on a sugar thermometer.

4 Meanwhile, whisk the egg white until
very stiff, but not crumbly, then slowly
drizzle the syrup into the egg white
while whisking constantly.

5 Quickly stir in the nuts and pour the
mixture into the prepared tin. Leave to
cool but, before the nougat becomes
too hard, cut it into squares.

CINNAMON AND ORANGE TUILES

THE AROMA OF CINNAMON AND ORANGE EVOKES A FEELING OF CHRISTMAS AND, SERVED WITH COFFEE, THESE CHOCOLATE-DIPPED TUILES ARE PERFECT FOR FESTIVE OCCASIONS.

SERVES FIFTEEN

INGREDIENTS
  2 egg whites
  90g/3½oz/½ cup sugar
  7.5ml/1½ tsp ground cinnamon
  finely grated rind of 1 orange
  50g/2oz/½ cup plain
    (all-purpose) flour
  75g/3oz/6 tbsp butter, melted
For the dipping chocolate
  75g/3oz plain (semisweet) chocolate
  45ml/3 tbsp milk
  75–90ml/5–6 tbsp whipping cream

1 Preheat the oven to 200°C/400°F/ Gas 6. Line three large baking trays with non-stick baking paper.

2 Whisk the egg whites until softly peaking, then whisk in the sugar until smooth and glossy. Add the cinnamon and orange rind, sift over the flour and fold in with the melted butter. When well blended, add 15ml/1 tbsp of recently boiled water to thin the mixture.

3 Place 4–5 teaspoons of the mixture on each tray, well apart. Flatten out and bake, one tray at a time, for 7 minutes until just turning golden. Cool for a few seconds then remove from the tray with a metal spatula and immediately roll around the handle of a wooden spoon. Place on a rack to cool.

4 To make the dipping chocolate, melt the chocolate slowly in the milk until smooth, then stir in the cream. Dip one or both ends of the biscuits in the chocolate and leave to cool.

COOK'S TIP
If you haven't made these before, cook only one or two at a time until you get the hang of it. If they harden too quickly to allow you time to roll them, return the baking sheet to the oven for a few seconds, then try rolling them again.

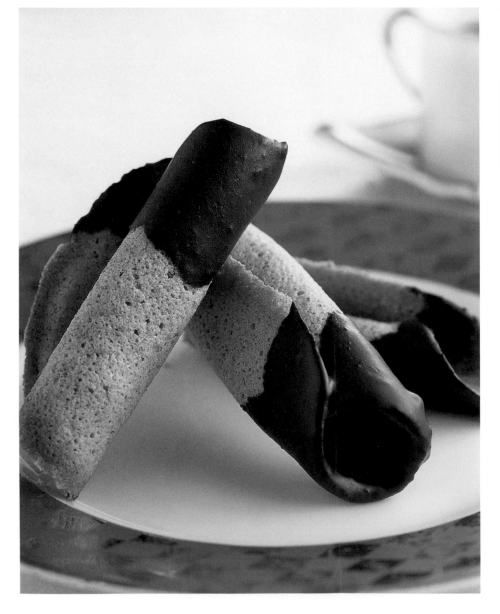

MINT CHOCOLATE MERINGUES

THESE MINI MERINGUES ARE PERFECT FOR A CHILD'S BIRTHDAY PARTY AND COULD BE TINTED PINK OR GREEN. ANY SPARES ARE DELICIOUS CRUNCHED INTO YOUR NEXT BATCH OF VANILLA ICE CREAM.

MAKES ABOUT FIFTY

INGREDIENTS
  2 egg whites
  115g/4oz/generous ½ cup caster
    (superfine) sugar
  50g/2oz chocolate mint
    sticks, chopped
  cocoa powder, sifted (optional)
For the filling
  150ml/¼ pint/⅔ cup double (heavy)
    or whipping cream
  5–10ml/1–2 tsp crème de menthe,
    or mint essence (extract)

COOK'S TIP
You can store these meringues in airtight tins or jars; they will keep for several days.

1 Preheat the oven to 110ºC/225ºF/ Gas ¼. Whisk the egg whites until stiff, then gradually whisk in the sugar until thick and glossy. Fold in the chopped mint sticks and then place teaspoons of the mixture on baking sheets covered with non-stick baking paper.

2 Bake for 1 hour or until crisp. Remove from the oven and allow to cool, then dust with cocoa, if using.

3 Lightly whip the cream, stir in the crème de menthe, and sandwich the meringues together just before serving.

CURD TARTS

THESE TASTY LITTLE TARTS, FROM THE NORTH OF ENGLAND, HAVE A LIGHT CURD CHEESE FILLING THAT SITS ON A TANGY LAYER OF LEMON CURD.

MAKES TWENTY-FOUR

INGREDIENTS
   450g/1lb shortcrust
    (unsweetened) pastry
   225g/8oz curd (farmer's) cheese
   2 eggs, beaten
   75g/3oz/generous ⅓ cup sugar
   5ml/1 tsp finely grated lemon rind
   50g/2oz/¼ cup currants
   60ml/4 tbsp lemon curd
   thick cream or crème fraîche, to serve

COOK'S TIP
Pastry freezes well. Save time by lining the tartlet tins (muffin pans) with pastry in advance, wrapping them in clear film (plastic wrap) and storing them in the freezer. When ready to cook, remove the tins from the freezer and allow to defrost for 1 hour, then fill and bake.

1 Preheat the oven to 180°C/350°F/ Gas 4. Roll out the shortcrust pastry thinly, stamp out 24 rounds using a 7.5cm/3in plain cutter and use to line patty or tartlet tins. Chill or set aside in a cool place until required.

VARIATION
For special occasions, add a drop of brandy to the filling.

2 Cream the curd cheese with the eggs, sugar and lemon rind. Stir in the currants. Place 2.5ml/½ tsp of the lemon curd in the base of each tartlet case. Spoon on the filling, flatten the tops and bake for 35–40 minutes, until just turning golden.

3 Serve warm or cold, topped with thick cream or crème fraîche.

ALMOND CREAM PUFFS

IN THESE LITTLE PIES, CRISP, FLAKY LAYERS OF PASTRY SURROUND A SWEET, CREAMY FILLING. THEY ARE BEST SERVED WARM, SO REHEAT ANY THAT BECOME COLD BEFORE EATING.

MAKES TEN

INGREDIENTS
275g/10oz puff pastry
15ml/1 tbsp plain (all-purpose)
  flour, plus extra
2 egg yolks
30ml/2 tbsp ground
  almonds
30ml/2 tbsp caster
  (superfine) sugar
a few drops of vanilla or
  almond essence (extract)
150ml/¼ pint/⅔ cup double
  (heavy) cream, whipped
a little milk, for glazing
sifted icing (confectioners')
  sugar, for sprinkling

1 Roll out the pastry thinly on a lightly floured surface, and cut out ten 7.5cm/3in rounds and ten 6.5cm/2½in fluted rounds. Keeping the smaller rounds for the tops, use the larger rounds to line a patty tin. Chill for about 10 minutes. Preheat the oven to 200°C/400°F/Gas 6.

2 Whisk the egg yolks with the flour, almonds, sugar and essence. Fold in the cream and spoon into the pastry cases. Brush the edges with milk, add the tops and seal the edges. Glaze with milk and bake for 20–25 minutes until golden. Cool slightly. Sprinkle with icing sugar.

FRESH FRUIT GENOESE SPONGE

GENOESE IS THE ORIGINAL FATLESS SPONGE, WHICH CAN BE USED FOR LUXURY GÂTEAUX AND SWISS ROLLS. IT SHOULD BE EATEN QUICKLY, AS IT DOES NOT STORE WELL.

SERVES EIGHT TO TEN

INGREDIENTS
oil or butter, for greasing
175g/6oz/1½ cups plain (all-purpose)
  flour, sifted
pinch of salt
4 eggs
115g/4oz/½ cup caster
  (superfine) sugar
90ml/6 tbsp orange-flavoured liqueur
For the filling and topping
600ml/1 pint/2½ cups double
  (heavy) cream
60ml/4 tbsp vanilla sugar
450g/1lb/4 cups fresh soft fruit, such
  as raspberries and strawberries
150g/5oz/1¼ cups shelled pistachio
  nuts, finely chopped
60ml/4 tbsp apricot jam (jelly),
  warmed and strained

1 Preheat the oven to 180°C/350°F/ Gas 4. Grease a 21cm/8½in round springform cake tin (pan), line the base with baking parchment and grease the paper with a little oil or butter.

2 Sift the flour and salt together three times, then set aside.

3 Place the eggs and sugar in a mixing bowl and beat with an electric mixer for about 10 minutes or until the mixture is thick and pale.

COOK'S TIP
If you wish to make the Genoese sponge a few days before you need it, it can be frozen. Allow to thaw at room temperature for several hours before filling.

4 Sift the pre-sifted flour and salt into the mixing bowl with the egg and sugar mixture, then fold together very gently. Carefully transfer the cake mixture to the prepared tin.

5 Bake in the centre of the oven for 30–35 minutes or until a skewer inserted into the centre of the cake comes out clean.

6 Leave the cake in the tin for about 5 minutes, then turn out on to a wire rack, peel off the lining paper and leave to cool completely.

7 Carefully cut the cake in half horizontally to create two layers. Place the bottom layer on a serving plate, then sprinkle the orange-flavoured liqueur over the cut side of each cake.

VARIATION
Because a Genoese sponge is made with no added fat, it makes a good choice for those who are watching their weight or following a low-fat diet. Replace the whipped cream filling with low-fat Greek-style yogurt and pile on the fresh fruit.

8 Place the double cream and vanilla sugar in a large mixing bowl and beat together with an electric mixer until the mixture stands up in peaks.

9 Spread two-thirds of the cream mixture over the bottom layer of the cake and top with half of the soft fruit.

10 Carefully place the second half of the cake on top of the layer of cream and fruit and spread the remaining cream over the top.

11 Arrange the remaining fresh fruit on top of the cake and sprinkle with the chopped pistachio nuts. If liked, lightly glaze the top layer of fruit with the warmed apricot jam, then serve.

FROSTED CARROT AND PARSNIP CAKE

THE GRATED CARROTS AND PARSNIPS IN THIS DELICIOUSLY LIGHT AND CRUMBLY CAKE HELP TO KEEP IT MOIST AND ACCOUNT FOR ITS VERY GOOD KEEPING QUALITIES. THE CREAMY SWEETNESS OF THE COOKED MERINGUE TOPPING MAKES A WONDERFUL CONTRAST TO THE CAKE'S LIGHT CRUMB.

SERVES EIGHT TO TEN

INGREDIENTS
  oil, for greasing
  1 lemon
  1 orange
  15ml/1 tbsp sugar
  225g/8oz/1 cup butter or margarine
  225g/8oz/1 cup light brown sugar
  4 eggs
  225g/8oz/1⅔ cups carrot and
    parsnip, grated
  115g/4oz/1¼ cups sultanas
    (golden raisins)
  225g/8oz/2 cups self-raising
    (self-rising) wholemeal (whole-
    wheat) flour
  5ml/1 tsp baking powder
For the topping
  50g/2oz/¼ cup sugar
  1 egg white
  pinch of salt

1 Preheat the oven to 180°C/350°F/ Gas 4. Lightly grease a 20cm/8in loose-bottomed cake tin (pan) and line the base with a circle of baking parchment.

VARIATION
If you do not like parsnips, you can make this cake with just carrots, or replace the parsnips with the same weight of shredded courgettes. Add a pinch of cinnamon and nutmeg to the mixture to give a little extra flavour.

2 Finely grate the lemon and orange. Put about half of the rind, selecting the longest shreds, in a bowl and mix with the caster sugar. Arrange the sugar-coated rind on a sheet of greaseproof paper and leave in a warm place, to dry thoroughly.

3 Cream the butter and sugar until pale and fluffy. Add the eggs gradually, then beat well. Stir in the unsugared rinds, the grated carrots and parsnips, 30ml/ 2 tbsp orange juice and the sultanas.

4 Gradually fold in the flour and baking powder, and tip into the prepared tin. Bake for 1½ hours until risen, golden and just firm.

5 Leave the cake to cool slightly in the tin, then turn out on to a serving plate.

6 To make the topping, place the caster sugar in a bowl over boiling water with 30ml/2 tbsp of the remaining orange juice. Stir over the heat until the sugar begins to dissolve. Remove from the heat, add the egg white and salt, and whisk for 1 minute with an electric beater.

7 Return to the heat and whisk for about 6 minutes until the mixture becomes stiff and glossy, holding a good shape. Allow to cool slightly, whisking frequently.

8 Swirl the cooked meringue topping over the cake and leave to firm up for about 1 hour. To serve, sprinkle with the sugared lemon and orange rind, which should now be dry and crumbly.

COOK'S TIP
When this cooked meringue frosting cools, it becomes slightly hard on the outside. The cake will keep well for a few days until the crust is cut into.

...ND SAFFRON BREAD

...E A GREAT ALTERNATIVE TO PLAIN TOAST FOR BREAKFAST OR TEA. SPREAD THIS
...ER WHILE IT IS STILL WARM FROM THE OVEN, OR SERVE AS BUTTERED TOAST.

MAKES TWO 450G/1LB LOAVES

INGREDIENTS
  oil, for greasing
  flour, for dusting
  150ml/¼ pint/⅔ cup, plus
    15ml/1 tbsp milk
  several threads of saffron
  60ml/4 tbsp clear honey
  450g/1lb/4 cups white (bread) flour
  5ml/1 tsp salt
  ½ sachet easy-blend (rapid-rise)
    dried yeast
  3 eggs
  60g/2¼oz/4½ tbsp unsalted (sweet)
    butter, melted and cooled

1 Lightly grease and flour two 450g/1lb loaf tins (pans). Heat half the milk with the saffron in a small pan until the colour seeps out of the saffron threads. Stir in the honey and set aside to cool slightly, then add the rest of the milk.

VARIATION
To make a richer loaf, add raisins or chopped dried apricots. This rich dough also freezes very well. Cook the loaves as above for 20 minutes, then reduce the heat to 180°C/350°F/Gas 4 for a further 15 minutes. Remove from the oven, cool, then remove from their tins, wrap well and freeze. To serve, defrost for about 2 hours, then bake in an oven preheated to 200°C/400°F/Gas 6 for 20 minutes, glazing if necessary.

2 Sift the flour and salt into a large mixing bowl, mix in the dried yeast and make a hollow in the middle.

3 In a separate bowl, beat together two eggs plus one extra yolk and pour into the flour along with the melted butter and cooled milk. Using a fork, work the egg into the flour until the mixture begins to come together.

4 Turn out on to a lightly floured surface and knead gently until you have a silky, soft, smooth, elastic dough.

5 Return the dough to a clean, lightly greased mixing bowl. Lightly grease the surface of the dough and cover the bowl with a clean cloth. Set aside in a warm place and leave for about 2 hours until doubled in bulk and very spongy.

COOK'S TIP
If you find that you have kept the bread for too long and it has become slightly stale, make into breadcrumbs and store in an airtight container in the freezer. They can be used to make a crisp coating for fish.

6 Turn the dough out on to a floured surface and knead it well until it is smooth and firm again. Divide into four pieces and shape into smooth round balls. Place them side by side in the prepared tins and set aside in a warm place to double in size again.

7 Preheat the oven to 200°C/400°F/Gas 6. When ready to bake, whisk the remaining egg white and use to glaze the bread. Bake for 35 minutes.

8 Check the bread to make sure it is not browning too quickly, and cover with foil if necessary. Cook for a further 10–15 minutes or until well risen, golden and sounding hollow when tapped underneath. Cool on a wire rack.

GREEK EASTER EGG BREAD

TOPPED WITH BRIGHTLY COLOURED EGGS, THIS ATTRACTIVE PLAITED BREAD IS AN IMPORTANT PART OF GREEK EASTER CELEBRATIONS. THE RED COLOUR USED TO DYE THE EGGS IS THOUGHT TO HAVE MAGICAL PROTECTIVE POWERS.

MAKES ONE LOAF

INGREDIENTS
  oil, for greasing
  450g/1lb/4 cups unbleached strong
    white (bread) flour, plus extra
  2.5ml/½ tsp salt
  5ml/1 tsp ground allspice
  2.5ml/½ tsp ground cinnamon
  2.5ml/½ tsp caraway seeds
  20g/¾oz fresh yeast
  175ml/6fl oz/¾ cup lukewarm milk
  50g/2oz/¼ cup butter
  40g/1½oz/3 tbsp sugar
  2 eggs
For the coloured eggs
  3 eggs
  1.5ml/¼ tsp bright red food
    colouring paste
  15ml/1 tbsp white wine vinegar
  5ml/1 tsp water
  5ml/1 tsp olive oil
For the glaze
  1 egg yolk
  5ml/1 tsp clear honey
  5ml/1 tsp water
For the decoration
  50g/2oz/½ cup split almonds,
    slivered (sliced)
  edible gold leaf (optional)

1 Lightly grease a baking sheet. First make the coloured eggs. Place the eggs in cold water, bring to the boil and boil gently for 10 minutes. Lift out of the water and place on a wire rack to dry. Mix together the red colouring, vinegar and water in a shallow bowl, then roll the eggs in the mixture. Return to the rack to cool and dry completely.

2 When the eggs are cold, drizzle the olive oil on to kitchen paper, lift up each egg in turn and rub all over with the oiled paper.

3 To make the dough, sift the flour, salt, allspice and cinnamon into a large bowl. Stir in the caraway seeds.

4 In a jug (pitcher), mix the yeast with the milk. In a bowl, cream together the butter and sugar, then beat in the eggs. Add the two mixtures to the flour and gradually mix to a dough.

5 Turn out the dough on to a lightly floured surface, and knead until smooth and elastic.

6 Place the dough in a large oiled bowl, cover with oiled clear film (plastic wrap) and leave to rise in a warm place for about 2 hours, or until doubled in bulk.

7 Knock back (punch down) the dough and knead on a lightly floured surface for 2–3 minutes. Return to the bowl, re-cover and leave to rise again for about 1 hour, or until doubled in bulk.

8 Knock back the dough and turn out on to a lightly floured surface. Divide into 3 equal pieces and roll each into a 38–50cm/15–20in long rope. Plait (braid) these together.

9 Place the dough on the prepared baking sheet and push the dyed eggs into the loaf. Cover and leave to rise in a warm place for about 1 hour.

10 Meanwhile, preheat the oven to 190°C/375°F/Gas 5. Combine the egg yolk, honey and water, and brush over the loaf. Sprinkle with almonds and gold leaf, if using. Bake for 40–45 minutes, or until golden and hollow sounding. Transfer to a wire rack to cool.

INDEX